D1710927

THE GREEK LANGUAGE
IN ITS EVOLUTION

THE GREEK LANGUAGE IN ITS EVOLUTION

AN INTRODUCTION TO ITS SCIENTIFIC STUDY

by

ANATOL F. SEMENOV

LONDON
GEORGE ALLEN & UNWIN LTD.
MUSEUM STREET

First published in 1936.

Printed in Great Britain by Stephen Austin & Sons, Ltd., Hertford.

CONTENTS

33007

PART II

AN HISTORICAL SURVEY OF GREEK SYNTAX

APPENDIX

PREFACE

The author of this little book intended to compose a short, but nevertheless complete, sketch of the development of the Greek language from the most ancient to its modern form, as it is spoken by the Greeks to-day. If he has had the courage to undertake this difficult task, it was because he desired to supply a need, which he himself had felt as a student of philology. So this work may well be dedicated to young students.

Although a great number of books dealing with the historical development of Greek have been published, it may be said that no work exists offering to students a *complete sketch* of this development *in the narrowest compass*. Such books as the excellent work of A. N. Jannaris are rather intended for professors than for students.

How far this attempt has succeeded let those who know judge. In any case the author was candidly animated by a sincere wish to offer to young scholars of philology a useful introduction to the history of an important language of the civilized world.

It is the author's agreeable duty to express here his hearty thanks to Professor R. M. Dawkins at Oxford and to Professor Rudolf Pfeiffer at Munich, who have generously helped him, when he was preparing his work for the Press.

ANATOL SEMENOV.

ROSTÓV ON DON.

INTRODUCTION

Die Entwickelung der Sprache illustriert die politische
und kulturelle Entwickelung eines Volkes.

The political and cultural development of a people is
illustrated by the development of its language.

[WILHELM HUMBOLD.]

A historian of the Greek language, as well as the historian of every other language, must represent all the phenomena observed in it in all the periods of its existence. As the language is continually changing, we may speak in a certain sense of its life as of the life of an organism. It has been born of single sounds[1] uttered by the first man (*homo primigenius*) or by separation from some other already existing language, which reminds us of the propagation by way of partition of certain living organisms. Once born the language grows.[2] Its forms and expressions become richer and more various conformably to the progress of the civilization. Here also an interesting analogy with living organisms may be mentioned. In the course of time old cells fall off to be replaced by new ones, in the same way during the development of a language certain words and expressions grow old, fall off, and are replaced by newly-formed

[1] These sounds were already articulated, for thus the human language differs from the sounds uttered by animals.

[2] Max Müller prefers to speak of the *growing* of a language, not of its *living* (Lectures on the science of language).

13

words and expressions. For example, in all languages a phenomenon commonly called deterioration is very well known. Already in the Attic of ancient Greek the word πονηρός we find only used with the meaning ' bad ' although its first meaning was ' painful ', as is shown by its common root with πονέω = to exert oneself. In Middle High German the word *diu wip* signifies ' woman ' in general, whilst in Modern High German the same word [1] has the contemptuous suggestion of a strumpet. In its first meaning the word is replaced by another: *die Frau.*—We may trace the analogy with living organisms still farther. As during the life of a living organism changes are due to the decrepitude of old cells and the formation of new ones, so in the life of a language not only words and expressions constantly change, but also the constituent parts of single words, the sounds and the suffixes. These are replaced by others. For example, the suffix νω in Modern Greek verbs has ousted many others: δύνω in place of δύω, μισθώνω in place of μισθόω, σπέρνω in place of σπείρω.[2] The evident consequence of such a process is that at last the language is changed to such a degree, that compared with its first form it appears to be something quite new,

---

[1] *Das Weib.* Mark also the change of the gender: neuter instead of the feminine.

[2] On the change of the language in general cf. L. Radermacher, *Neutestamentliche Grammatik*[2] (Tübingen, 1925), chap. iii, Wirkende Kräfte der Sprachentwickelung.

just as in the butterfly we fail to recognize the caterpillar. The language in its first form has ceased to exist; it is in a certain sense dead. It must be granted, that we cannot often speak of dead languages in the strictest sense of the word, that is of languages which are no longer spoken by any people. We may speak of such only when the people itself has died out, as in the case of some American and Australian tribes, or when it is absorbed by another people, as was the fate of the ancient Etruscans. In general they continue to live in their descendants developed from them in consequence of the metamorphosis mentioned above. Latin continues its life nowadays in the languages of the so-called Latin peoples: Italian, Spanish, Portuguese, French, and Romansh. As for Greek, the close affinity of the language of modern Greek, with the language of Homer, notwithstanding the great difference, is quite undeniable. There is even a movement among the καθαρίζοντες to write and to speak, if not the ancient Ionic dialect, at least the language of the Hellenistic period, the so-called κοινή, although with certain concessions to the living speech. If generally Ancient Greek and Latin are called dead languages, that may be admitted only in the sense that they are not spoken by any people nowadays in their pristine purity.

Turning now to the special study of Greek, we observe in the first place, that, as we have already suggested, it has not always presented the same features. From the literary monuments preserved to us from different periods we observe a continual change of the language in its sounds, roots, expressions, meaning and forms of words, and lastly in syntax. The causes of these changes were various. The change of the sounds and of the syntax was doubtlessly influenced by contact with the languages of foreign peoples, although this influence must not be exaggerated, for sounds in the course of time are of themselves subject to organic changes. As for the change of the meaning of words, we can point to the following causes: (1) Nouns and verbs irregularly declined and conjugated are replaced by regular ones; the ancient substantive φρέαρ (genitive; φρέατος instead of φρέαρος) is replaced nowadays by the regularly declined πηγάδι(ον)—gen. πηγαδίου. In a similar manner the verb οἴομαι = ' I think ' is replaced by the regular verb πιστεύω = I believe (credo). (2) Replacement by a synonym: ποιῶ (= I do) is replaced by κάμνω (= I have pain in doing something). (3) Religious causes: Greeks say ψωμί(ον) = bread-crumb instead of ἄρτος (= bread) because this word is now used especially for the bread of the Communion. (4) Some words are replaced by others, because they have preserved only one particular meaning. For example, καλός signifies now only ' good.' In the meaning ' fair ' it is replaced by ὡραῖος (= properly ' ripe ').

Although the changes of the language never happen suddenly, but always slowly and by degrees, we may divide the whole development of Greek into certain periods. In each of these the language had its particular colour, as for example the sea has different colours as the light varies. These periods are: *Ancient Greek*, *Hellenistic Greek* or κοινή (scl. γλῶσσα), *Vulgar Greek* or the Greek spoken in the Middle Ages, and *Modern Greek*. But we must emphatically remark, that in dividing the history of Greek in such a manner we mean only the spoken language, for we observe that in Greek, more than in other languages, the literary language has always remained in its development behind the spoken. The poems of Homer were composed in a language which was already antiquated when they appeared. The people of Attica in the 5th and 4th centuries before Christ spoke another language than that, which we find in the works of Plato, as is proved by contemporaneous inscriptions. In the 2nd century of our era Plutarch and Lucian were still writing the Ancient Attic, although in daily conversation they certainly used the κοινή of their time. Even the authors of the Byzantine period sometimes used the same antiquated dialect. And modern educated Greeks often intermingle their language with old words and forms of words dead long ago, or else they speak and write the ancient κοινή and modify it with new words and forms. This is the so-called

B

καθαρεύουσα or γραπτὴ διάλεκτος, an artificial product, which first appeared about the year 1700. Modern conceptions unknown in antiquity are nevertheless expressed by means of ancient Greek words. The cravat is called λαιμόδεσμος and the bicycle ποδεηάτης, although the people use the foreign words κραβάτα and βελοσιπέ.

Besides changes due to the progress of time, we observe in Greek, as in other languages, contemporary differences of sounds, words, and forms of words corresponding to the difference of the tribes, into which the nation has been always divided. In all periods we have to deal with a great number of Greek dialects. Their difference one from another in phonetics, in morphology, in syntax, and in vocabulary is often very great, but nevertheless the language always preserves the same general aspect. It would hardly be possible in a given case to doubt whether we are dealing really with a genuine Greek dialect. If we say cautiously ' hardly ', we are thinking of one exception: the dialect of the ancient Macedonians. It is known to us very imperfectly. We have only some single words preserved to us by the ancient lexicographers. At any rate, the dialect was closely related to Greek. But at present we cannot positively say whether it was an independent *language* or only a *Greek dialect*. This question will be treated below. Here we can only say that the Macedonian did not observe the phonetic laws, by which the Greek is distinguished from other languages of the Indo-European group.[1]

[1] See below.—Th. Bergk, O. Hoffmann, J. Beloch, and G. Hatzidakis were sure that the Macedonian was Greek. Bergk believed that it was an Aeolic dialect, whilst Herodotus (v, 6) declares the Macedonians to be ancestors of the Dorians. Ottfried Mueller called them Illyrians (*Ueber Wohnsitze der Makedonier*, 1825). Hirt and Thumb are of opinion that in Macedonia two languages were spoken : the dominant class of the inhabitants were Greeks, whilst the subjects were Illyrians (= Albanians). Fick, too, called the Macedonians Semi-Hellenes (Halbgriechen). Cf. Kazarow in the *Revue des études grecques*, 1910, p. 21.

PART I

THE FORMS OF THE GREEK IN THE COURSE OF TIME

CHAPTER I

GREEK IN ITS RELATION TO OTHER LANGUAGES

It is natural that before we proceed to the particular study of a certain branch of science, we should first of all accurately mark out its extent. In the present case our first task will be to mark out the limits of Greek, that is to point out what is its principal difference from other languages. It is evident that we are here speaking only of such languages as are next of kin to the Greek, the languages of the Indo-European group.

It is well known that in related idioms similar words are found. We must seek for strict rules, that we may be able in each case to say with certainty that the word in question is really Greek.

Such a rule may be derived from the observation that to single sounds of other languages certain fixed sounds in Greek correspond.

Further, the forms of words in related idioms are nearly identical, but in each they are recoined in a peculiar manner. It is therefore clear that in order to determine exactly the limits of Greek we are obliged to compare the phonetics and the morphology of this language with those of each of the other Indo-European languages. If we were actually to do this with each language, it would be an extremely tiresome task. But it is now proved that if we strip off the individual differences of phonetics and flexion of idioms belonging to the same family, the phonetics and flexion of one language can be reconstituted, which was the forefather of all these idioms.[1] Thus it is sufficient to compare the phonetics and flexions of Greek with those of the primitive Indo-European language to find out the characteristic features of this idiom. In doing so we obtain the following results.

By the comparison of languages comparative philology has established that the primitive language of the Indo-Europeans possessed besides the vowels, which occur in all modern languages, certain other vowels, which later have become consonants. These are the nasals and liquids: r, l, m, and n. To mark them as vowels we use: $r̥$, $l̥$, $m̥$, and $n̥$.[2] It was quite natural that as soon as these vowels became consonants other vowels

[1] Of course, we have no right to suppose that this primitive language can really be reconstituted at the present day *in its full form*, as some scholars have hoped. The reason for this is that many phenomena of the phonetics and flexion cannot be ascribed to any precise period. The French scholar Laurand has very suitably observed that if Latin were to be lost, we should not be able to reconstitute it by means of the modern Roman languages.

[2] Osthoff, in *Pauls Beitraege zur Geschichte der deutschen Sprache* (3, 32), was the first to ascribe to the primitive language a syllabic $r̥$. Brugmann did the same for the nasals (*Curtius Studien*, 9, 287). Sometimes these sounds are written as r, l, m, n, but this may lead to a confusion with the so-called 'cacuminalia'.

should develop themselves beside them in order to make them audible. Now the usual vowel for this in Greek is α. Before consonants we find here in lieu of ŗ αρ or ρα : κραδίη, καρδία, cf. the Slavonic *srŭdice*.—Before vowels αρ appears exclusively : καρῆναι from the stem kŗ.—The long r̄ appears as ρα or ρω; cf. in Sanscrit c̄irša—the head (stem kȳ̄); στρωτός; cf. in Sanscrit *stirnás*. —The short ļ before consonants appears as αλ or λα : ἀμαλδύνω; cf. the Latin *mollis* from *molduis (stem mļdu).—Before vowels in place of ļ αλ appears: παλύνω (stem pl). The long l̄ appears as λα or λω: λᾶνος; cf. the Latin *lāna* and the Slavonic *vŭlna* (stem uļn); cf. in Sanscrit *mūrdhán* (stem mļdh).—The short m̥ before consonants appears as α: ἑκατόν; cf. in Sanscrit *çatám* and the Latin *centum* (stem km̥tom).— Before vowels it appears as αμ : ἅμα; cf. the Gothic *sums* and the German *samt* (stem sm̥).—The long m̄ appears as μᾱ: δματός, in Ionic δμητός; cf. in Sanscrit *dāmyati* (stem dm̄).—The short n̥ before consonants appears as α: αὐτόματος; cf. the Latin *commentus*; δασύς, cf. the Latin *densus* (stem dn̥); ἄ-δηλος (stem n̥).—The short n̥ before vowels appears as αν: ἀν-όρυχος = not fortified (a privativum); cf. the German *un-befestigt*.—The long n̄ appears as νᾱ: γνητός (from *γνατός), cf. the Gothic *kuni* (= the tribe). Stem is gn̄.

There is a still more important test, by which

genuine Greek words may be distinguished from words in related languages. The mediæ (aspirated or not) appear in Greek as tenues aspiratæ. The Sanscrit word *dhuma*, the Slavonian *dym*, and the Latin *fumus* appears in Greek as θυμός (θ = *th*, where *t* and *h* are pronounced separately). We may compare the Sanscrit *bhu*, the Latin *fu* (in *fui*), the Slavonian *by* (in *by-tj* = to be), and last but not least the English ' be ' with the Greek φύ-ω (*p-hyo*). The Slavonian word *mglá* appears in Greek as -ὀ-μίχλη (*o-mikhle*).

The *j* in the beginning of the words of the primitive language appears in Greek as the spiritus asper ; but if this sound was preceded by a media aspirata, the sound appeared as ζ. The Sanscrit word *jaj* corresponds to the Greek ἅγιος; *judh* = ' to fight '—to ὑσμίνη (= battle); *jah*—to ὅς; *jusmá*—to ὑμεῖς. But the Sanscrit *jusá* (cf. the Russian *ukhá* = a fish-soup) corresponds in Greek to ζωμός; *jugá* (cf. the Latin *iugum* and the Russian *igo* = yoke) to ζυγόν; *Djauḥ* to Ζεύς (cf. also the Latin *Juppiter* from *Juh-pitar = Ζεὺς πατήρ).

The sibilant *s* initial before a vowel and between two vowels appears in Greek as the spiritus asper. Later it disappears totally: in Sanscrit *súdas* (cf. the Latin *sedes*)—in Greek ἕδος; in Latin *sarpo* (cf. the Slavonian *sr̥p*)—in Greek ἅρπη ; in Sanscrit *saptá* (cf. in Latin *septem*)—in Greek ἑπτά; in Latin *muris* (genitive from *mus*)—in

Greek μυός (from *μυσός, *μυhός); in Latin *generis* (genitive from *genus*)—in Greek γένεος (from *γένεσος, *γένεhος). It must be granted that there are also apparently exceptions to this rule, but they are only seeming. For instance, the σ between two vowels has not disappeared in the word Ποσειδών.[1] But here the σ was not original. It has developed itself from ὶ by the so-called palatalization. The original form of the word was *Ποτενς-δάν (cf. the Latin *potens* and the Sanscrit *pati* = the master). The same may be said of φασί (from *φατί). In the form ἔστησα the σ was preserved by the analogy of such forms as ἔτυπ-σα.

To the gutturals of the primitive language, when followed by *j* or *y*, ττ and σσ correspond in Greek: in Sanscrit *pacyaté* (from *peqjo*)—in Greek πέσσω (cf. in Russian *pekú* from the infinitive *péçj*), in Sanscrit *ca-*, in Greek τε (from ττ); in Sanscrit *laghú*—in Greek ἐ-λάσσων (from *ἐ-λαγηjων).

The sounds *dh* + *j* appear in Greek as τσ and σσ: in Latin *totus* from *totjos* (cf. the genitive *totius*)—in Greek: τόσσος and τόσος; in Sanscrit *madhya*; in Latin *medius*; in Russian *mézdu* (= between); in Greek—μέσσος or μέσος (from *μέδηjος).[2]

With regard to the accent of words in Greek,

---

[1] It is true that in Laconia we meet the form Ποὶδόν, but the spiritus has appeared here by analogy with other cases, where σ is found between two vowels and passes then to the spiritus.

[2] On the relation of Greek sounds to the Indo-European, cf. Giuseppe Ciardi, *Appunti di fonologia greca*, Firenze, 1923.

there is the rule of the three syllables, which beside Greek exists only in Latin; only one of the three last syllables of a word is accentuated; but here this rule was not observed before the 3rd century before Christ.[1]

In Greek morphology first of all as a peculiar feature the ending of the superlative τατος must be mentioned. Further we observe as peculiarities the pronoun ἐ-κεῖνος (κῆνος and τῆνος in Dorian countries) and the following verbal forms: (1) the perfect with κ (πεπαίδευ-κ-α); (2) the aorist passive in θε; (3) the imperative middle with the ending σθω.

These are the principal features by which a genuine Greek word may be distinguished from similar words in the related languages. There still exists a doubt about the dialect of the ancient Macedonians. Was this language actually a form of Greek? Were the Macedonians Greeks? To-day it is still more difficult to reply positively to this question, than in antiquity, when the doubt already existed. We hear that King Alexander I of Macedonia was not allowed to partake in the games at Olympia for the reason that he was not a Greek (Herodotus, v, 22). But the same author— Herodotus—declares that the Macedonians were next of kin to the Greek tribe of the Dorians (v, 56; viii, 43). Hellanikus traced the descent of

---

[1] We infer that the accent of 'áfficio' stood originally on the fourth syllable from the end, because otherwise the word would be 'affácio'.

the Macedonians from Æolus like the Greek tribe
of the Æolians (cf. Stephanus of Byzantium, s.v.
Μακεδονία). For us the difficulty lies in the fact
that we possess not a single text of any length
in the Macedonian dialect. We know only some
proper names and some words preserved to us by
the Greek lexicographers.[1] We observe a strange
mixture of Greek and non-Greek elements. The
words γαβαλά or κεβαλή (cf. the Slavonian glava
and the Russian golowá, the German Giebel, and
the English ' gable ' in another sense), ἄγημα,
ταγός (from τάσσω) seem to be Greek; but γάρκα
(a wand ; Bergk compares the Latin virga),
ἄβαγνον (the rose), κοῖδος (the number; according
to Bergk = ταμίας and kin to the Latin s-cindo)
are scarcely Greek. Not Greek, but at least Indo-
European words are: γόδα (the bowels; cf. the
Sanscrit gudam = the gut), ἀργίπους (the eagle;
cf. the Sanscrit rjipjáh), ἴλεξ = the Latin ilex.
We may infer a foreign admixture in the
Macedonian, although it was a Greek dialect. It
is known that in the lines of the Greek poet
Hipponax we meet many foreign words (χλούνης =
the robber, πάλμυς = the king, βεβρός = good). He
lived in Asia Minor on the border of non-Greek
nations. In the same way in Macedonia, which
was a border-country where different nations met

[1] Cf. Sturz, De dialecto macedonica, 1809 ; A. Fick, Orient und
Occident, and in Zeitschrift für vergleichende Sprachforschung,
22, 193 ; Gustav Meyer in Jahrbücher für Philologie, 1875, 185 ;
O. Hofmann, Die Makedonen, Göttingen, 1906.

(Illyrians, Thracians; it appears that even the non - Indo - European Etruscans were formerly neighbours of the Macedonians), the Greek had not preserved its proper purity. In examining the question, it is important to consider if in Macedonia the Greek phonetic laws just mentioned were regularly observed. We observe that the mediæ aspiratæ of the primitive language do not appear in Macedonia as tenues aspiratæ, as in Greek, but as tenues and mediæ. For instance, the Sanscrit *bhruvah* and the Greek ὀ-φρύες in Macedonian, according to the ancient authors, was ἀβροῦϜες or ἄβροτες, that is probably ἀ-βροῦϜες, because *T* and *F* are often confounded in the tradition (cf. the Slavonian *brŭvi* and the Russian *bróvi*). Although in the Avesta, as it must be granted, we meet the stem with a *t*: *brvathyam*, similarly in old Irish: *bruad*. Further cf. the Greek θώραξ and the Macedonian δώραξ; the Greek θανών and the Macedonian δανών. The Macedonian name Γαιτέας is probably derived from the Greek Χαίτη. Instead of Φερενίκη the Macedonians said Βερενίκη, and instead of Φίλιππος—Βίλιππος. In the papyri found in Egypt we meet the Macedonian names Βίλιος = Φίλιος and Λόβιος = Λόφιος.

Our conclusion is that Macedonian stood in a relation to Greek as Dutch stands to German. It was a language directly akin to the Greek, but not a dialect of the latter. The educated classes spoke probably a pure Greek.

If Greek had among the other Indo-European languages a quite independent position and its territory may be closely defined, the question may well be put, whether it was not particularly related to one of the other languages.[1] In Antiquity the opinion prevailed that the Greek was next of kin to the Italian languages, especially to Latin. It was even said that the latter was a dialect of Greek. Also many modern scholars have held that these two languages were in close relation to one another. This was the opinion of such renowned scholars as Theodor Mommsen, Ernst Curtius, and Heinrich Kiepert. To-day this opinion has been entirely abandoned. Carl Lottner in *Kuhns Zeitschrift für vergleichende Sprachforschung* (vii, pp. 18–49, 160–193) was the first to protest against it. Greek seems rather to belong to the eastern Indo-European languages. Some phonetic and morphological phenomena do indeed show a certain affinity with the Italic languages.[2] For instance, the mediæ aspiratæ appear as tenues aspiratæ in Italic as in Greek (the primitive *bh* as *ph*, etc.). Further, the genitive of the plural of the *A*-stems has adopted the ending of the pronominal flexion of the primitive language: *āsōm.* (Cf. θεάων = **deāsōm-dearum.*) In

---

[1] On the reciprocal relation of the Greek to other languages, cf. Athanasios Buturas, *Ein Kapitel der historischen Grammatik der griech. Sprache*, Leipzig, 1910.

[2] Cf. A. Meillet et Vendryes, *Traité de grammaire comparée des langues classiques*, Paris, 1924. V. Henry, *Précis de la grammaire comparée du Grec et du Latin*, Paris, 1896.

the first and second declension we find on both sides the ending of the dative instead of the original ending of the locative, and in the third declension we find, on the contrary, the locative instead of the dative. (Cf. λύκῳ *lupo*, πόληϊ *siti*.) Lastly, Greek belongs to the group of the so-called centum-languages, like the western languages. We meet in Greek the guttural *k*, where the eastern satem-languages show a sibilant.[1] One might compare the Sanscrit *daça*, the Armenian *tasn*, the Lithuanian *deszimt*, the Russian *djésjatj*, and on the other side the Latin *decem* (*dekem*), the Gothic *taihun*, and the Greek δέκα; further, the Russian *çudo* (= the miracle) and the Greek κῦδος; the Sanscrit *śvan*, the Armenian *sun*, and the Greek κύων (the Latin *canis*). But on the other side in Greek, as in the East, to the labio-velars *qu* and *gu* of the western languages corresponds the simple guttural *quis* in Latin, κίς in Greek (in Ionic; in other dialects τίς). As in some eastern languages, we meet in Greek the augment: in Sanscrit *a-bharat*, in Armenian *e-ber*, in Greek ἔ-φερε. With regard to stems Greek often occupies a quite isolated position, not joining either the western or the eastern group. The word ' sea ' (in Latin *mare*, in

[1] This main difference between the phonetics of the western and eastern Indo-European languages was shown by T. v. Bradke (*Methode der arischen Altertumswissenschaft*, p. 64). But nowadays this division of the Indo-European languages is not generally accepted. According to the wave-theory of J. Schmidt it is to be considered that single members of the two great groups could cross one another.

Slavonic *more*, in German *Meer*) is expressed in Greek by a series of words, not one of which contains the stem *mar*: θάλασσα, πέλαγος, πόντος.[1] For the word ' corn ' the Greek has no expression at all (in Latin *granum*, in Gothic *kaurn*, in Russian *zernó*). A certain affinity of the Greek with the Iranian and some languages of Asia Minor may be observed, as the Phrygian and the Armenian.[2] It is very probable that in early times the Greeks were neighbours on one side of the Arijans (Iranians and Indians) and on the other, of the Italic peoples.[3]

Notwithstanding its distinct individuality Greek has never been averse from receiving foreign elements. Advancing towards the South into the country later called Hellas, the Greeks found it already occupied by several nations. In Thessalia they met the Pelasgians. Their capital was Larissa. This country later was called Pelasgiotis (χώρα Πελασγιῶτις). The nation was widely spread, if we may believe the testimonies of ancient authors. The Odyssey mentions Pelasgians living in Crete. Herodot. tells us that they were settled in Attica

[1] Properly = way ; cf. the Sanscrit *pánthāh*, the Latin *pont-s*, and the Slavonic *putj*.

[2] Hübschmann in *Kuhns Zeitschrift*, 23, 49, has proved the affinity of the old Phrygian with the Armenian. Also the old Thracians in the north of Greece were akin to the Phrygians, and consequently to the Armenians.

[3] Herodot. (vi, 45) relates that in his time (5th century B.C.) Βρύγοι = Φρύγες were still living in Macedonia. Even in the heart of Hellas, on the border of Boeotia and Attica, Thucydides (ii, 22) mentions a city named Φρύγια. Thucydides mentions also Thracians in Phocis (ii, 29). That they lived in Boeotia is proved by the myth of Semele (in Phrygian ζεμέλω = the earth).

and in a part of the Peloponnesus (in Achaia and in Arcadia. Herodot. i, 146 ; vii, 94). Further, according to the same author, in Thrace (Kreston) there existed still in the 5th century before Christ a Pelasgian settlement. They lived also in Lemnos, Imbros, Samothrake, in Chalcydike, on the Propontis (Herodot. i, 57).[1]

The question, who the Pelasgians really were, is one of the most difficult questions of Greek prehistory. Among modern scholars Eduard Meyer and Julius Beloch have identified the Pelasgians with the oldest *Greek* colonists. It is probable that πελασγός or πελαργός signified simply ' very old ', a transport of the primitive meaning ' grey ' (cf. πολιός and Kretschmer, *Einleitung in die Geschichte der griechischen Sprache*, p. 160),[2] that is that the word ' Pelasgians ' would be a collective designation of all prehellenic tribes in Hellas and it would signify ' the oldest inhabitants '. But against such an interpretation it must be observed that Homer (τ. 175–7) and Herodot. expressly mention a ' pelasgian language ' as different from Greek. Thucydides declares the Pelasgians of Lemnos and *Etruscans* (iv, 109) of Attica to have been Tyrrhenians. Indeed, Pauli and Lattes

---

[1] On the settlements of the Pelasgians in Greece, cf. Ottfried Mueller, *Etrusker* (2nd edition, 1877).

[2] It is known that the crane in Greek is named πελαργός, because of its grey feathers. Other derivations of the word πελασγοί have been proposed : from πέλας—οἱ πέλας οἰκοῦντες = neighbours, or from πέλαγος—πελαγίσκοι = men living on the shore. (Cf. Crain in *Philologus*, x, p. 577.)

(*Rendiconti del Istituto Lombardo* 40 (1907), pp. 815 sq.) believe that an inscription in an unknown language found on Lemnos is Etruscan. Also Sophocles (cf. Dionysios of Halicarnassus, i, 25) knew of *Etruscan* Pelasgians.

We hear also of many other nations in Greece: Lelegians, Carians, Dryopians, Cauconians, Abantians, etc. Although they were early pushed away by the advancing Hellenes, and some emigrated while others were absorbed by the newcomers, we may suppose that some words of their languages, as they lived sometimes in close contact with the Greeks, passed into the language of the latter.

Further, the fact is not to be neglected that in some districts of ancient Greece the Semitic Phœnicians had founded their settlements. Their presence in Crete is proved by old rituals and Semitic names of places and rivers.[1] It was possible that some semitisms may have penetrated into Greek, but the number of Semitic words in Greek was formerly much overestimated. Many have proved themselves on closer observation to be Indo-European (cf. A. Mueller in *Bezzenbergers Beitraege*, i, 273, and—less radically—H. Lewy, *Semitische Lehnwörter im Griechischen*). But the

---

[1] *Iardanos* (cf. the river Iordan in Palaestina), *Itanos* (= a stronghold, from the Semitic *eithan* = strong), *Salmonion* (from *salom* = peace). The name Iardanos we find beside Crete, also in Elis (H 135). The tribe of the Γεφυραῖοι in Attica descended from Phœnicians (Herodot. v, 5).

existence of a certain quantity of Semitic words in
Greek cannot be doubted. It is characteristic that
for the most part they are names of articles of
importation, or in general, of things connected
with trade: χιτών (Semitic *chetoneth*, a piece of
linen. This stuff the Greeks first knew from the
Semites having made use before only of wool),
μύρρα, σινδών (*sadin* = a linen cloth), μνᾶ, χρυσός (in
Hebrew: *charun*), κάδος, κῆβος (in Hebrew: *qob*),
σάκκος, κάνεον. Everybody knows that the names
of the Greek letters are also Semitic.

To what great groups of nations the nations living
in the prehistoric Greece belonged, with the
exception of the Phœnicians, we do not know.
We have no idea of their languages as not one text
has been preserved to us. Modern scholars suppose
the existence of a peculiar group of languages,
which was neither Semitic nor Indo-European,
spoken on the shores of the Mediterranean Sea.
It has been observed that many of the names of
old cities and countries in Asia Minor, which are
not intelligible to us, have certain endings, which
reappear also in the names of some cities and places
in ancient Greece. H. Kiepert (*Lehrbuch der alten
Geographie*, pp. 73, 90) was the first who turned
his attention to the endings ισσος, ασσος, ησσος
(ηττος), ωσσος, ινθος, and υνθος; for instance,
Ἁλικαρνασσός, Λυρνησσός, Σαγαλασσός, Μύλασα,
Ἄρπασα, Βάργασα, Λάρισσα (in Mesopotamia). The
Greek local names Λάρισσα (in Thessalia), Παρνασσός,

Κνωσσός, Κηφισός, Ὑμηττός, Κόρινθος may be compared.[1] We find in Greek not only local names with these endings, but also other words: κυπάρισσος, ἀσάμινθος, λαβύρινθος (from *λαβράυνδος, λάβρυς = the axe, which symbol is often found painted on walls of the old palaces in Crete), ὑάκινθος. We know now that in the old Luwian (a branch of the Hittite in Asia Minor) the suffixes nt and ss had the meaning 'belonging to'.[2] Further, we find words in Greek which cannot be traced either to an Indo-European or to a Semitic origin. We observe that these words are usually names of things belonging to a relatively high degree of civilization. For instance, the words for stone-buildings are not of Hellenic origin. The Greek and Indo-European word δόμος (in Latin: domus) means not a house, but a primitive wooden hut. Similarly οἶκος (Ϝοῖκος; cf. the Latin vicus) means only a dwelling in general. The names of actual stone-buildings in Greek are not Indo-European: πύργος, θάλαμος, θόλος, τύρσις (τύρρις; cf. turris). The ending of θάλαμος we find in a word we meet in Asia Minor—Πέργαμος, whose root is identical with the root of πύργος. The word τύρρις reminds us of the nation of the Tyrrhenians or Etruscans (Τυρρηνοί, Τυρσηνοί, *Τύρσκοι, *Tursci, Tusci, *E-tursci, Etrusci), which nation lived, it seems, in

---

[1] Cf. A. Fick, Vorgriechische Ortsnamen, Göttingen, 1905.
[2] On the Greek words with the suffixes νθ and σσ cf. also W. G. Arkwright in Journal Hell. Stud. 38 (1918) : 'Lycian and Phrygian names.'

Greece also, and was not Indo-European.[1] The name of the bath-tub, an object of higher civilization, was not a Greek word; the ending μινθος of ἀσάμινθος points again to Asia Minor. Also the words τερέβινθος, λέβινθος, ἐρέβινθος must be mentioned in this connexion. Further, modern scholars have observed that ῥόδον, βασιλεύς, ἄναξ, μίνθη, λείριον are not Greek, but 'Ægean'. Even the names of the Greek gods often prove themselves not to be Greek, but of foreign origin.[2] The word ᾿Αθάνα (᾿Αθήνη is the Ionic form, and the Attic form ᾿Αθηνᾶ—from **᾿Αθηναια—is a Greek amplification of the original word) has the same ending as the name of the prehistoric town Mycene (Μυκᾶναι). The name of the well Πιράνα at Corinth also may be compared.[3] Many other names of Hellenic gods are also not Greek : ῎Αρης, ῎Αρτεμις, ῞Ηφαιστος, ᾿Απόλλων (cf. the Assyrian word *apalu* = to prophesy).

We may conclude that from very early times there were in Greek many foreign words. J. Hubert (in *De lingua antiquissimorum Graeciae incolarum* Commentationes Aenipontanae) (1921) has counted over 550, which he believes the Greeks took over from the earliest inhabitants of Greece. Many of these were not even Indo-European. Sometimes when the root of a Greek word appears to be Indo-

---

[1] But it must be mentioned that the Albanese of our days are also named ' Toscs ' (Hahn, *Albanische Studien*).

[2] Already Herodot. (i, 57) supposes that the names of the Greek gods were Egyptians.

[3] Staehlin in the ᾿Αντίδωρον for Wackernagel (1923) compares the suffix *na* with *na* in *kinaahi* = Chanaan. Cf. Wilamowitz, *Athena, Sitz. Ber. d. Berliner Akademie*, 1921, 950.

European, it is not certain that the word is really
Indo-European. The root of the word Φοῖνος is
found in other languages of the Indo-European
group (in Latin *vinum*; in German *Wein*; in
Slavonian *vinó*). The primitive form is *vaina*; but
we meet the same root also in the Hebrew word
jajin. Further, we may compare the Greek ταῦρος
(primitive form: **staura*—in Latin *taurus*, in
German *Stier*, in English ' steer ') and the Semitic
tauru; the Greek λέων and the Assyrian *labbu* (the
Hebrew *labhi*), the Greek χίλιοι (from **χεσλιοι*),
and the Semitic *gharuta* and *harudu*. It is probable
that such words were borrowed by both primitive
Indo-European and primitive Semitic from some
third language. But Hommel (in *Die Namen der
Saeugethiere*, pp. 260, 414) supposes these words
to be very old words common to both Indo-
European and Semites of the period when they
belonged to the same group of nations.[1]

[1] Of some interest is the fact that the inflexion of substantives
is sometimes even in Finnish like the Indo-European and the
Greek flexion : *maas-sa* = in the earth (cf. the Indo-European
ending *su* or οι in ᾿Αθήνησι), *maas-ta* = from the earth (cf.
θεν), *maah-an* = to the earth (cf. the ending of the accusative
m = *am* = *an*), *maal-le* = on the earth (cf. θεν and δε in
ἔρασδε). Cf. K. B. Wiklund in *Monde Oriental*, 1906, pp. 51–2 ;
Paasonen, *Finnisch-ugrische Forschung*, 1908 ; Nicol. Anderson,
*Studien zur Vergleichung der ugro-finnischen und indoeurop.
Sprachen*, Dorpat, 1897. It may be mentioned also that words
occur in Greek, as in some other Indo-European languages, which
show a remarkable affinity with Finnish words (Tomaschek,
*Übereinstimmende Wörter der finnisch-ugrischen und indo-
germanischen Sprachen* : Wiener Akademie, phil.-hist. Klasse
(Bd. 96 und 117) : (old Latin *cluo*), cf. in Finnish : *kuulen
(kulen, kolam)*—ὄνομα (from ὄ-νομα ; in Latin *nomen*)—*nimi*—
ὕδωρ (from the root *vud* ; cf. in Sanscrit *udan*, in Slavonian
voda) *wesi*—μέθυ (in Sanscrit *madhu*, in German *meth*)—*mesi*.

CHAPTER II

GENERAL SURVEY OF THE DIALECTS OF
ANCIENT GREEK [1]

It is well known that the language of a people,
just as much as the archæological evidence, is an
important source for the study of its earliest
history. When we study the Greek language, we
observe that the nation before entering the country
called Hellas had already completely formed its
characteristic individuality. But it is also evident
that the occupation of the territory did not take
place all at one time, but by successive advances,
single groups of the nation detaching themselves
from the bulk and making their progress independently. These groups had then for a long while
a separated existence and lived each its own life.
This we deduce from the fact that Greek never
presents itself to us as a unity, but always split
into a certain number of dialects. Already the
language of Homer, the oldest specimen of Greek
preserved to us, presents a mixture of different
dialects. From the 7th century before Christ,
i.e. from the earliest time when we have specimens
of the language in the form of contemporary

[1] O. Hofmann, *Die griech. Dialekte in ihrem histor. Zusammenhang*, Göttingen, 1891-8.

inscriptions, we can observe the existence of a great number of local dialects. Wackernagel estimates this number to be about thirty (*Ueber Geschichte der griechischen Sprache*, Goettingen, 1913). Some variation in phonetics or in the flexion of words being limited to a narrow area had no influence upon the bulk of the language. The variety of local particularities was always growing.[1] But already the ancient authors had observed that the mass of local dialects could be reduced to a small number of groups, each offering certain characteristic particularities. The distribution of the Greek dialects into three groups conforming to the division of the nation into three principal tribes— the *Dorian*, the *Æolians*, and the *Ionians*—is very old. But already in the 1st century of our era Strabo made out *four* groups: to the just mentioned three groups he added the *Attic*. The dialects which could not be ascribed either to the Dorian or to the Ionian group, he ascribed to the Æolian. But in this other ancient scholars did not entirely agree with him. Strabo assigned the Ætolians and Epirotes to the Æolian group, while Stephanus Byz. (s.v. ʼ*Ιωνία*) and the grammarian Meermannianus (ed. Schaefer, p. 642) placed them

---

[1] In the formation of the dialects, according to the opinion of many scholars (Johann Schmitt, Max Mueller, A. Pictet, Fr. Spiegel, etc.), this *wave-like* movement played the most important part. But also a mutual influence *by leaps* is to be observed. The form of the name of *Ζεύς-Τâνα* is found in Crete and Elis, as ʼ*Οράτριος* instead of *Ϝράτριος*. This may be explained by intercourse by sea.

among the Dorians. Clemens of Alexandria added
to Strabo's four dialect groups a fifth dialect, the
so-called κοινὴ διάλεκτος, a language used after the
formation of Hellenistic kingdoms in the 4th
century before Christ by the more intelligent
Greeks, which by degrees ousted all the other
ancient local dialects (Stromateis, i, 21, 172). These
died away and the last official documents written
in local dialects are dated from the 2nd century
of our era.[1] But out of the κοινή as spoken by the
majority of the nation new dialects were born, and
from these the modern dialects are derived.

The opinion of modern scholars in regard to the
groups of the ancient Greek dialects differ from
those of the ancient authors. There is, for example,
no doubt that the Attic cannot be separated from
the Ionic group. Further, those dialects which
cannot be ascribed either to the Doric or to the
Æolic group, but present characteristic features
of both, have been united to form a new group.
As these dialects were at first regarded as a
particular kind of Doric, they have been called
pseudo-Doric (as Pezzi did) or north Doric (according to Hoffmann). Nowadays they are named
Greek of the north-west, as Brugmann proposed.

As for the Æolic dialects, it was long ago

[1] The gradual extinction of the old Greek dialects is well
illustrated by the statistical table drawn by A. Thumb (in *Die
griech. Sprache im Zeitalter des Hellenismus*, p. 48). For example,
the frequency of the Æolic O instead of the a of common Greek
(ὀν instead of ἀνά, στροτός instead of στρατός) is in the 4th
century B.C. 4 : 7, in the 3rd 2 : 18, and in the 2nd 1 : 22.

observed that they do not form precisely a unity. Ahrens distinguished a genuine (Lesbos, Thessalia, Boeotia) and a pseudo-Æolic or not purely Æolic subdivision (Arcadia and Elis) of this group. Hirt has conjectured that the separation was a result of the advance of the Dorian tribes (*Gr. Laut und Formenlehre*, p. 35). Doubt has recently been cast even upon the close kinship between Lesbian and Boeotian. The latter seems to be connected rather with the western dialects (Dorian in the widest sense). Similarly the dialect of Elis forms a transition from the purely Doric to the Greek of the north-west. Arcadian, which is identical with Cyprian, is related to Lesbian as well as to Triphylian. Instead of Æolic the expression ' Central Greek ' is now used and, as in antiquity, four groups of Greek dialects are distinguished, although they are not identical with the groups of Strabo. These groups are: (1) An Ionic-Attic group; (2) West Greek (Dorian); (3) North-west Greek; (4) Central Greek. Subdivisions of the last are: (*a*) the northern group (Lesbos, Thessalia); (*b*) the southern group (Arcadia, Cyprus, Pamphylia). Subdivisions of the Ionic are: (*a*) the dialects of Asia Minor and (*b*) the Attic. But A. Thumb in his work on this subject, *Die griechischen Dialekte*, proposes to distinguish only three groups: (1) *The Western or the Dorian group* in the widest sense with the subdivisions: (*a*) Dorian dialects properly so-called; (*b*) the dialect of Achaia; (*c*) the dialect of Elis; (d) the North-west Greek. (2) *The Central Greek group* (the Æolic or the old Achaian dialects) with the subdivisions: (a) the Œolic (the Thessalian and Lesbian dialects); (b) the Arcadian and Cyprian dialects; (c) the Pamphylian dialect. (3) *The East Greek group* with the subdivisions: (a) the Ionic; (b) the Attic.

The heroes of the oldest Greek epic poems known to us call themselves Achæans. The ancient authors thought that this tribe was identical with the Æolians (cf. Anonymus, quoted by Strabo, p. 333). In Æolic Cyprus we hear indeed of an Ἀχαιῶν ἀκτή. According to the Hittite texts found at Boghazköj in Asia Minor, the Ajavalas (the Αἰϝολεῖς) were a principal tribe of the Akhijava (the Ἀχαιοί).[1] On the other hand, R. Meister believed the Achæans connected with the Dorians and J. Beloch plainly put them down as Dorians, because the Peloponnesian Achæans of historical times as well as the Achæans of Phthiotis in Thessalia spoke Dorian, as is evident from their inscriptions (*Griech. Geschichte*, i, 2, p. 90).

In consequence of the natural formation of the country, Hellas is divided into many districts. As intercourse between these regions was very difficult in antiquity, the roads being very bad, the language in each of them developed separately. It must be added, that through the prehistoric

---

[1] The King of Lazpa (= Lesbos) in the 14th century before Christ was subject of the King of the Hittites (cf. Drerup in the *Phil. Wochenschrift*, 1926, col. 229).

separation of the Greek tribes, the language of the
first inhabitants of any district was bound to be
mixed with that of the newcomers. Therefore, if
we try to assign to the dialect of a region of ancient
Greece its proper place in the scheme of dialects
mentioned above, we often find ourselves at a loss.
Thus the region of Argolis in the Peloponnese must
be counted among Dorian regions; but in the
inscriptions we find besides Dorian forms Æolic
ones. Further, the dialect of Elis belongs to the
north-west Greek group, but in the inscriptions of
the southern part of this region, we find almost
exclusively Æolic forms of words. Also generally
we find in the Dorian inscriptions of the Pelo-
ponnese many Æolisms, for example $\pi\epsilon\delta\acute{a}$ instead
of $\mu\epsilon\tau\acute{a}$ and $\acute{\epsilon}s$ instead of $\acute{\epsilon}\xi$. Even in Laconia:
$\acute{\epsilon}\pi o\acute{\iota}\eta\hbar a$ instead of $\acute{\epsilon}\pi o\acute{\iota}\eta\sigma a$. These facts may be
easily explained if we recollect that the Dorians,
when they reached the Peloponnese, mixed with
the former Æolic or Achæan and partly also with
Ionian inhabitants. Of the distribution of the
Greek dialects in the territory of Hellas before the
Dorian invasion, the following sketch may be
traced.

The Dorians [1] lived in northern Epirus, the
southern part being occupied by the Eleans. The
Ionians inhabited besides Attica, Eubœa and

---

[1] $\varDelta\omega\rho\iota\epsilon\hat{\iota}s$ from the stem $\delta o\rho\digamma$; cf. $\delta\acute{o}\rho\upsilon$ = spear, but
originally = wood, tree. Cf. the Slavonian ' drevo ' = tree,
and the Russian ' derevo ' = wood or tree. Further, the name
of the tribe ' Drevljáne ' in old Russia.

Bœotia (here close to the Æolians); also Megara and the northern part of the Peloponnese: Corinthus, the Argolis, and north-eastern Arcadia. We find here in the inscriptions residues of their dialect: the particle ἄν instead of κεν or κα, the conjunction εἰ instead of αἰ, the infinitive with the ending ναι instead of εν. The northern Æolians occupied Thessaly, Phocis, Locris, and a part of Bœotia. The southern Æolians had wandered from Thessaly to the Peloponnese, where they became neighbours of the Ionians in Achaia, Elis, Messenia, Laconia, and western Arcadia. By degrees they pushed the Ionians completely out of the Peloponnese. They settled in Crete, Cyprus, in the Sporades, and in the islands formerly occupied by the Ionians and named, therefore, Ionian islands: Zacynthus, Kephallenia, and Ithaca.

In consequence of the Dorian invasion the distribution of the Greek tribes and of their dialects underwent another change. The purely Dorian tribe of Bœotians, which had its name from the mountain Boîon in Epirus, where it had lived before, invaded Thessaly. Pushed forward in their turn by the Æolian Thessalians, the Bœotians together with the Æolians coming from the southern Thessaly invaded first Phocis and afterwards the territory which then acquired the name of Bœotia, where naturally a mixed Dorian-Æolian dialect was formed. Portions of the other Dorian tribes of northern Epirus also emigrated, being oppressed by the Illyrians (Albanians). As they were not able to get footing in northern and central Greece (except in the little territory of Doris), they continued their march southwards. In the Peloponnese, which they reached by way of the Isthmus and perhaps by crossing the Corinthian gulf, they occupied Achaia, Megara, Messenia, Argolis, and Laconia. Together with the Dorians Ætolians and Eleians reached the Peloponnese. That the Eleians had lived before in Thessaly is proved by the existence of the name Olympos in this region and of the name Olympia in Elis. Further, Ætolian forms of words (as παίδοις instead of παισί) in the Eleian dialect prove that Æolians settled by the side of the Eleians. In the Peloponnese the Æolian dialect was preserved only in Arcadia, though not in its pure form, many Ionic forms being mixed with it. In consequence of the Dorian invasion the Æolians of Arcadia found themselves separated from their kinsmen in the island of Cyprus.

From the Peloponnese or perhaps directly from central Greece [1] the Dorians came across the sea to the island of Crete, afterwards also to other islands in the southern Ægean Sea: Cythera, Rhodus, Cos, etc. The number of the immigrants

[1] It is supposed that a part of the Dorians reached Crete directly from central Greece by sea. In Crete τσ has passed to ττ, whilst the Peloponnesian Dorians changed τσ to σσ.

must have been very considerable, for the islands in later times were completely doricized. Only particularities of the Doric spoken in Crete are left to remind us of the former Æolian inhabitants. For example ὄνυμα instead ot ὄνομα, οἱ instead of the Dorian τοί; the endings οισι and αισι of the dative plural, the prepositions ἐς instead of ἐξ, ἰν instead of ἐν, πεδά instead of μετά. Advancing from the islands the Dorians occupied also the adjacent shore of Asia Minor.

From the Peloponnese were ejected not only the Æolians, but also the remnant of the Ionians. These turned to the east and occupied some islands of the Ægean Sea: Paros, Naxos, etc. Then they reached the shore of Asia Minor. Here they again met the Æolians, who this time were not able to stand against them. Æolic cities and islands became Ionic: Erythræ, Clazomenæ, and the island of Chios.[1] In this region, where both groups of dialects had in some period existed one by the side of the other, the immortal poems of Homer originated, the language of which shows a mixture cf Ionic and Æolic. That is to say we have already a literary dialect, in which, in order that it may be intelligible not in a single district only, but generally, no one dialect is allowed a

---

[1] Remainders of the Æolic were here : αἰ = εἰ, πρήξοισι, λάβωισι, ἐσλός = ἐσθλος, *IGA*. 382, 1. There was also a tendency to a southern extension of the Ionians. Halicarnassus, formerly a Doric city, became Ionic. Herodot., a Halicarnassian, wrote his history in Ionic.

position of predominance. In general, too, the want of a commonly intelligible language was deeply felt in Greece. In order to remedy this want, local dialects were very shortly formed. Neighbouring tribes in particular felt the need of some means of inter-communication. Often the origin of such artificial dialects was political. As is known, the states of the Peloponnese formed a Union under the presidency of Sparta. Intercourse between the leading district and the members of the Union had to be in a language commonly intelligible. In consequence, a literary Doric dialect was formed, for most of the Peloponnesian states were then Doric. Traces of this language are found also outside the Peloponnese in Crete and Sicily. Another case is the powerful Athenian League, which was formed at the time of the Persian war and was a formidable rival to to the Peloponnesian League. In all their common intercourse the members of this League made use of a language which was intelligible to all of them, and this was the dialect of the town, which stood at the head of the League, the Attic, the dialect spoken at Athens. But after the political ruin of Athens this dialect preserved its dominant position, because of the great influence and prevalence of the Attic literature. Even Alexander the Great and the ' Diadochi ' composed their official documents in the purest Attic. At the same time, we may observe in the relation of

Attic to the Ionic dialects of the islands the working of the well-known law of physics, that action and reaction are equal. Ionic forms of words crept into Attic. We find, for example, in the 3rd century before Christ σσ instead of ττ (μέλισσα instead of μέλιττα), γίνομαι instead of γίγνομαι. Thus a new Attic-Ionian was born. Beside this mutual influence, entirely new forms appeared: the aorist εἶπα was formed instead of εἶπον on the analogy with the termination of the perfect in α. This new dialect was called the ' common dialect '—κοινὴ διάλεκτος—because it was from this time in common use of the Greek society especially in the kingdoms of the ' Diadochi '. But also in Greece it ousted little by little the local dialects including even its grandfather—the Attic. As for the latter, a reaction followed: from the 1st century of our era the pure Attic was again used, at least in literature. But as this dialect had already been forgotten by the majority of the nation, Attic dictionaries were then composed, some of which have been preserved to the present day, for example, the dictionary of Moeris and that of Phrynichus.[1]

While in the mouth of the majority of the people the language was ceaselessly developing and changing, an influential part of the lettered classes

[1] In the 4th century of our era Attic was already dead. It was learned only in schools. In a papyrus published in the fifth volume of the *Berliner Klassikertexte* a professor of the school at Berytos is specially praised for his knowledge of Attic.

was doing its best to stop this progress. They continued to make use of old forms of words and expressions dead long since. While on the basis of the Attic-Ionic dialect and the κοινή new dialects were forming themselves, out of which a new κοινή, i.e. the modern Greek, was developed, the learned minority obstinately adhered to the use of the dead Attic. Out of this latter with certain concessions to the living language there sprang about 1700 the so-called καθαρεύουσα (διάλεκτος or γλῶσσα). An educated modern Greek of to-day has three native-tongues: ἡ δημώδης διάλεκτος, the καθαρεύουσα, and finally the old κοινή. But it must be remarked, that a part of the educated public is of opinion that in the literature the καθαρεύουσα, to say nothing of the old Attic, ought to be replaced by the living δημώδης or χυδαία διάλεκτος. This linguistic question has provoked innumerable learned treatises and books, and has been discussed with the greatest ardour. There have been on both sides renowned philologists and literary men. On the side of the καθαρεύουσα stood, for example, Hatzidakis and Pecz, and on the side of the δημώδης—Psicharis and Krumbacher. At any rate, everybody who wishes to study modern Greek literature in its original language must know both forms of the language, the καθαρεύουσα and the δημώδης, for authors make use sometimes of one and sometimes of the other.[1]

[1] The journals are printed in the καθαρεύουσα.

It has been remarked that the dialects of modern Greek have developed out of the old spoken κοινή. They have no relation to the ancient Greek dialects, which already in the 2nd century of our era had disappeared almost entirely. This disappearance may be well studied in the inscriptions, although we must not forget that popular dialects lived much longer than literary dialects. For example, in the official and for the most part non-official German literature, the High-German prevails, whilst the dialects still live among the people.

But to the derivation of the modern Greek dialects from the ancient κοινή one interesting exception must be noted: the dialect of the so-called Zakonians, a tribe living in the ancient Cynuria in the Peloponnese or Morea. According to the statement of Philippson [1] the number of the inhabitants of this territory is 9,000 persons living in seven villages. But Ornstein estimates this number far less: only 1,000 persons. The territory of Cynuria is the south-eastern corner of Argolis, where this latter borders upon the ancient Laconia, and the Zaconian dialect seems to be a direct descendant of the old Laconian,[2] though this has sometimes been contested. Instead of the word σκυλί(ον) used in modern Greek [3]

---

[1] Petermann's *Mitteilungen*, 1890, p. 38.

[2] Thumb derives Τσάκων from ὁ ἐξ Ἀκωνίας (λ disappears before dark vowels). Deffner derives Τσάκωνες from τοὺς Ἄκωνες.

[3] From σκύλαξ in ancient Greek.

and meaning ' the dog ', the Zaconians say: Kue =
Κύων like the ancient Greeks conserving the pronunciation of the υ as U (= u in ' full '), not as
Y or I (= i in ' still '), as in modern Greek. This
letter was pronounced in this way also in old
Laconian. Similarly the Zaconians pronounce
ψυχή—psjucha (not ' psykhi '), and ' the bad
wife ' is in Zaconian ἁ κακὰ γουναῖκα. We observe
the conservation of α, as in ancient Laconian.
The affinity of the Zaconian with this dialect
becomes still clearer, if we observe the passing of
θ into σ,[1] which was characteristic of Laconian.
For example, the word θέρος is in Zaconian *séri*,
κριθά—*krisá*. Further, the change of the sibilant
into an aspirate is to be observed in σκ and στ,
which become *kh* and *th*: ἄκho (over ἄκκορ) =
ἀσκός, ἔτhε = ἔστε. Instead of ἐκεῖνος we find
ἐτῆνε = old Dorian (ἐ)τῆνος. Very characteristic
is also the rhotacism in the endings of words
followed by a vowel: καλέρ = καλός, or *tar ameri* =
Τᾶς ἁμέρας = Τῆς ἡμέρας. Before consonants ρ
is omitted: *kalé, dabelé* (= δαβελός = δαλός). The
old digamma is preserved in the form of β.

Nevertheless, many scholars still doubt the
derivation of Zaconian from the ancient Laconian.
Even the Hellenic origin of this tribe has been
contested It has been declared Slavonic [2] or

---

[1] Only before *i* and *e*, according to Pernot. Cf. Deffner,
Zakonische Grammatik.

[2] As for the origin of the modern Greek nation in general the
theory of Fallmerayer is well known (*Fragmente aus dem Orient,*

Altaïc. The French scholar Hubert Pernot (in *Revue des Etudes Grecques*, 1910, janvier–février) has attempted to prove that the Zaconian is a purely modern dialect of the Greek. If in Zaconian ' I am ' is ἔνι [1] and not, as usually in modern Greek, εἶμαι, he thinks that this form is not to be compared with the old Laconian ἠμί, but that it is only an analogy to the third person ἔνι. The first person of the plural ἔμε has no relation to the old Laconian ἠμέρ (= ἠμεῖς), but is a transformation of the modern form εἴμεθα into the active form ἔμε(ν), etc. In a similar manner also Psicharis, and before him Leake, try to explain the Zaconian forms of words by the modern Greek ones.

We suppose that the Zaconian is a mixture of all these elements.

1877) that it is a mixed people of Illyrians and Slavonians. Constantinus Porphyrogenneta (De them, 53) says : ἐσθλα-βώθη πᾶσα ἡ χώρα (the Peloponnese) καὶ γέγονε βάρβαρος. In the 15th century still Σθλαβῖνοι are mentioned in the Peloponnese (Morea). The word ' mother ' in Zaconian is *mati* as in Slavonian languages. Cf. Kopitar in *Wiener Jahrbücher für Litteratur*, 1822 (17, p. 96), and Gregorovius, *Stadt Athen*, i, 117. The Venetians called the eastern coast of Morea—Sclavonia. Cf. *Acta Sanctorum*, 8 iulii, p. 504 : urbem Manabaziam in slavinica terra. But Miklosic (Wiener Akademie, 1870 : *Die slav. Elemente im Neugr.*) has proved that in the modern Greek language are very few Slavonic elements. Bernh. Schmidt (*Das Volksleben der Neugr. u. das hell. Altertum*, 1871) has proved that the pagan elements met within the Christian religion of the modern Greeks directly descend from the antiquity. Cf. also J. C. Lawson, *Modern Greek Folklore and Ancient Greek Religion* (1919).

[1] The letter ν is pronounced *nj*.

CHAPTER III

A DETAILED ACCOUNT OF THE DIALECTS OF ANCIENT GREEK

As we have seen above, we may distinguish in ancient Greek the following great groups of dialects: (1) the Æolian or Achæan (called by Thumb Central Greek); (2) the Dorian; (3) the north-western Greek (these two groups sometimes called also western Greek); and (4) the Ionic-Attic group. But besides these groups it was not long before literary forms of the language containing elements from more than one dialect were developed. The literary language of epic poetry (called simply epic dialect) contains many Æolic forms, although in general it is an old form of Ionic. It has even been supposed that the poems of Homer, our oldest specimen of the epic dialect (as of Greek in general), were composed originally in pure Æolic. The German scholar, A. Fick, has made the experiment of translating them back into the supposed original dialect. The truth is that Homer and other epic poets made use of ancient Æolic heroic ballads and have preserved some words and expressions in their original form. At any rate, all Greek epic poets have since that time written in this mixed dialect. The Greek elegy having arisen from epic poetry, the elegiac poets wrote in the same dialect. Similarly, the dialect of Attic tragedy has a peculiar language in consequence of the use of occasional Ionisms and Dorisms. In general it must be observed that the Greek dialects influenced one another. In their unsullied purity they can be studied only in some official documents preserved to us in the form of inscriptions on stone or metal. The oldest document of this kind is the treaty between the Eleians and the Euvaœans dating from the year 570 before Christ.[1] This document engraved on a plate of bronze is composed in pure old Eleian. The numerous Greek official documents written on papyrus, which have been found in Egypt, are not composed in the ancient local dialects, but in the official language used from the times of Alexander the Great, the κοινή (διάλεκτος).

Our next task is to distinguish the characteristic features of each of ancient Greek dialects. But we must always remember that this can be done only roughly, because, in consequence of reciprocal influences, the most various shades of dialects were in use inside each group. In the relatively small territory of the Ionian colonies in Asia Minor four different dialects, according to the testimony of Herodotus, could be discovered. The same might be said of modern Greek dialects. On the island of Chios Psicharis found four different dialects.

[1] So dated by Kirchhoff in *Geschichte des griech. Alphabets.*

I. The Æolian or Achæan Group

To this group the following single dialects must be ascribed : (*a*) Thessalian (with the exception of the dialects of Thessaliotis and Phthiotis, which belong to the north-western group); (*b*) Lesbian; (*c*) Arcadian; (*d*) Cyprian, and (*e*) Pamphylian. To these the ancient authors added also the Bœotian dialect, but this is rather a transition to the western Greek or the Dorian.

The Æolian group falls into two subdivisions: *northern Æolic* (Thessalian, Lesbian) and *southern Æolic*, where the influence of Ionic is observed (Arcadian, Cyprian, and Pamphylian).

The Phonetics

(1) The vowel α often appears as ο: βροχύς = βραχύς, δέκοτος = δέκατος, ἐφθορκώς = ἐφθαρκώς. Sometimes the ο was pronounced very narrowly and changed to U (= the English *u* in ' full '). It was then written υ; for example, ὄνυμα = ὄνομα, δεῦρυ = δεῦρο, ὔμοιος = ὅμοιος, ὔν = ὀν = ἀν (ὐνέθηκε = ἀνέθηκε). The long ω became also υ (= *u*); for instance, ἔδουκε (= ἔδωκε), τοῦν = τῶν, ἀπίτου = ἀπίτω.

(2) The diphthong αι and more rarely οι and ει lose their ι before a vowel: Μυτιληνα(ί)ων, πο(ι) ήσασθαι.

(3) The ε becomes ι—βορίας = βορέας, ἄγι = ἄγε.

(4) The syllable πο appears as πτο : πτόλεμος = πόλεμος. From this the Macedonian name Πτολεμαῖος is derived. The Macedonian was certainly influenced by the neighbouring Thessalian. In the text of Homer πτόλις = πόλις is one of the Æolisms of the poems. By assimilation πτο changes to ττο : ττολίαρχοι = πτολίαρχοι. But in the syllables τε and τει in the beginning of words and after a nasal consonant the τ becomes π: πεῖσαι = τεῖσαι, πέμπε = πέντε, πέσσυρες = τέτορες = τέτταρες. Similarly, δ becomes β: βελφίς = δελφίς, Βελφοί = Δελφοί.

(5) The syllables αρς and ρατ become ερς and ρετ : θέρσος = θάρσος, κρέτος = κράτος.

(6) The syllable βερ becomes μερ : κυμερῆναι = κυβερνᾶν.

(7) In northern Æolic the sibilant σ is assimilated to the following nasal or liquid : ἔμμι = ἐσμί = εἰμί (cf. the Slavonian jesmj and the Sanscrit asmi), ἄμμες = *ασμες (also in Laconia cf. the accusative asman in Sanscrit) = ἡμεῖς in Attic, ὔμμες = *jυσμες = ὑμεῖς in Attic, στέλλαι = *στέλσαι = στεῖλαι in Attic, ἀργεννός (in Homer) = *αργεσνος (cf. the adjective ἀργής).

(8) When after o the nasal ν falls out, it becomes οι, not ω or ου, as commonly : καλέοισι (from *καλέοντι), not καλοῦσι (from καλέουσι, as in Attic).

(9) In Southern Æolic the dental τ becomes σ : σις = τις. Instead of ε before vowels, ι has

developed and after this we find a *j*, as in modern
Greek: Ϝέπιja = ἔπεα (= ἔπη in Attic).

(10) In the Pamphylian dialect a metathesis
of the sound ρ is to be noticed: 'Αφορδίσιυς =
'Αφροδίσιος. The same phenomenon has been
observed in Crete: 'Αφορδίτα = 'Αφροδίτη, σταρτός
= στρατός, which points to an old Æolian coloniza-
tion of the island. Further, in Pamphylia and in
Crete θ becomes τ: ἄτρωπος or ἄντρωπος = ἄνθρωπος.

The ancient authors believed also that the
sound Ϝ (= English *w*), the so-called digamma
(the letter has the shape of a double gamma),
was a peculiarity of the Æolic dialects and therefore they spoke of a 'digamma æolicum'. But
the inscriptions teach us that this sound originally
existed in all Greek dialects. It may be granted
that the Æolians preserved it the longest.[1] We find
it in Crete as an Æolism in Dorian inscriptions
even in the 2nd century before Christ, when it
had long ago disappeared in the other dialects.
The Zaconians alone preserve it to-day in the form
of the occlusive consonant β (= English *v*).

A characteristic mark of the *Lesbian* dialect
among the other Æolian dialects is that the aspirate
is missing in the beginning of the words. This is
the well-known 'psilosis', which we remark also
in dialect-English (cf. ''at' instead of 'hat', ''is'

---

[1] But already in the 6th century before Christ in the lines of
Alcæus and Sappho the digamma is found only at the beginning
of words before ρ instead of the spiritus asper.

instead of ' his '). This peculiarity spread to the neighbouring Ionic dialects.

The Morphology

Instead of the endings as and ης of the nominative singular of masculine substantives of the first declension, we find in Æolic the ending α: νεφεληγερέτα (Ζεύς) instead of νεφεληγερέτης.[1]

The genitive singular of the first declension has the ending αιο, whence after the disappearance of the ι (between two vowels according to the universal rule) was formed αο and αυ; the latter ending we find in Argolis: τᾶς ἀγοραῦ (= ἀγορᾶς) = ἀγοραῖο = ἀγορᾶο.

Instead of the demonstrative ὅδε, we find in the Northern Æolic ὄνε, and in the South—ὄνυ or ὄνι.[2]

Instead of the indefinite pronoun τις, in the South we find σις.

The so-called verba contracta are conjugated without the theme and have the endings of the μι conjugation: κάλημι = καλέω. Some forms nevertheless preserve the theme: καλέοισι, ἀγρεόμενοι.

The infinitive of the aorist passive has the ending ην or θην, instead of ηναι or θηναι, for example: μεθύσθην = μεθυσθῆναι.[3] Perhaps this is

---

[1] Brugmann (*Grundriss der vergl. Grammatik*, ii, p. 651) declares that this form is a vocative.

[2] Cf. the Slavonic demonstrative ' onyi ' and the personal ' on ' = he.

[3] Cf. the lines of Alcæus: νῦν χρὴ μεθύσθην καὶ τινα πρός βίαν πώνην, etc.

due to the influence of the ending of the present active ην.

Instead of the preposition μετά (with genitive) the Æolians made use of πεδά. It was probably an ablative form from the stem πεδ (cf. the Latin stem *ped* in *pedis*—genitive of *pes*). As preposition the word signified 'step by step with somebody'.

In Southern Æolic we find the preposition πός instead of πρός, and ἰν instead of ἐν.

The conjunction καί appears in the South as κάς.

The Dorian particle κα is in Æolic κε or κεν (= the Ionian ἄν). In Arcadia we find ἄν as an old Ionism, for the country was originally occupied by Ionians. In Northern Æolic the dative plural of the third declension has under the influence of the εσ-stem the ending εσσι instead of εσι (cf. Τείχεσσι, originally Τείχεσι). The Æolism is usual in the epic dialect.

In the North the perfect participle has the ending ων instead of ώs: γεγόνων = γεγονώς.

In Southern Æolic the dative plural of the third declension has the ending οις, as in the second declension: παίδοις = παίδεσι = παισί.

Of the accent of Æolian words, the ancient authors tell us that it was drawn back as far as possible, which phenomenon was called βαρυτόνησις. We cannot verify this statement because in the inscriptions there are no accent marks and in the papyri the accents are indicated only sporadically. We must also remember that the literary fragments on papyrus, which have come down to us, have been revised by the Alexandrian scholars according to their own theories, which sometimes were wrong. Besides it is only from Lesbos that the barytonesis is reported.

The Bœotian dialect, as we have already said, occupied a position between the Æolic and the Doric or Western Dialects, but the proportional strength of these two elements varies widely from place to place. At Thebes the Dorian element was stronger than at Tanagra (cf. *Grammatici Græci*, iii, 469). Also in some parts of Thessaly a mixed dialect (Dorian-Æolian) was spoken, as is proved, for instance, by the inscription of Sotairos.

II. The Dorian (or Western) Group

The most characteristic feature of the Dorian dialects is their conservatism. We find here many sounds and forms, out of which evidently sounds and forms of other dialects have themselves developed. Of all the dialects Doric was nearest to the primitive Greek.[1]

The Phonetics

The most important principle is the preservation of the pure long *A* (= the English *A* in ' father ' or ' far '), which in Ionic became a mixed sound

---

[1] Max Müller (*Lectures on the Science of Language*, ii, p. 30) declares that Doric was a subdivision of Æolic. It must be granted that it was nearer to the Æolic than to the Ionic.

between A and E, like the English a in ' language '. In Ionic this sound was written H, η. We may compare the Dorian φάμα (= the Latin *fama*) and the Ionian φήμη.

The long A was predominant in Doric also in the contraction $o + a$; *πρό-ατος became in Doric πρᾶτος, whilst in Ionic we have πρῶτος. But $a + o$ became ω.

The short A in the ending of a word contracted with η or ε became η: ἐνίκη from *ἐνίκαε (in Ionic ἐνίκα).

The consonant τ never became σ as in other dialects: Ϝίκατι (not εἴκοσι), λέγοντι (not λέγουσι); cf. in Sanscrit *bodhanti*. But in the Dorian territory Argolis we find φέρουσι under the influence of Ionic.

The sound represented by the letter υ has preserved in Doric its primitive value of a pure u (the English u in ' bull '), whilst in other dialects it became an intermediate sound between u and i (like u in the French words *lune* or *prune*). Then the palatalization of the τ ensued as regularly before thin vowels: συ instead of τυ.

Morphology

The article (originally a demonstrative pronoun, Indo-European ' to ') in Doric preserves its t in the plural: τοι and ται instead of οἱ and αἱ of other dialects.

The substantives in ευς in flexion preserve their ε: βασιλέϜος, βασιλέϜι, βασιλέϜα (in Æolic βασιλῆϜος and in Ionic βασιλῆος [1]; after metathesis of quantity: βασιλέως.

The demonstrative ' that ' (in German *jener*, in Sanscrit *etēna*) was in Doric τῆνος instead of κῆνος = κεῖνος or ἐ-κεῖνος.

Beside the dative ἐμοί we find in Doric ἐμίν. The ending ιν corresponds to the ending *jam* of the locative in Sanscrit, Avesta, and Lithuanian.

The personal pronoun of the second person singular preserved in Doric its τ: τύ = *tu* in Latin, *du* in German, ' thou ' in English, *ty* in Slavonian. The dative is τεΐν (from τεϜjam; cf. in Sanscrit *tubhyam*), τιν, and τίνη [τιν + νή; νή = νά.—νή Δία]. Cf. in Russian *wot tebe Bog!* = Here to thee God, a form of assurance.

The infinitive of the athematic μι conjugation has in Doric the ending μεν or μην instead of ναι or Ϝεναι: δόμεν = δοῦναι (from *δο-Ϝεναι, cf. in Sanscrit *da-vane*), παιδευθῆμεν = παιδευθῆναι.[2]

The first person of the plural active has in Doric the ending μες instead of μεν. The primitive Indo-European form was *mas*.

The formation of the future with σε or σι instead of the simple σ (παιδευσέω, παιδευσῶ instead of

---

[1] But because of the abbreviation of the η before dark vowels, also βασιλέος.

[2] The ending μεν or μην is a contamination of μεναι and εν. This latter corresponds to the ending of the Sanscrit locative of the stems on *i* and *ū-ăm*. The ending μεναι in Homer and the Lesbian corresponds to the Sanscrit *manē* in *damanē*—a dative.

παιδένσω) corresponds to the Indo-European future formed by *si* or *sy* (cf. in Sanscrit *da—sy—ami*, in Lithuanian *busiu* = I will be).

The future passive has the endings of the active: συναχθησοῦντι, from συναχθησέοντι.

The verbs in ζ are conjugated with a guttural stem: ἐμέριξαν = ἐμέρισαν, δικάξεσθαι from δικάζεσθαι.

Of all the Dorian dialects the Laconian, the dialect of the old Spartans, is the most remarkable. A certain development may be observed: an Old-Laconian and a New-Laconian may be discerned.

The Old-Laconian: (1) ε before dark vowels changes to ι: ἀνιοχίων (= ἡνιοχέων), θιός = θεός. An influence of the old inhabitants of Laconia the Achæans or Æolians is generally supposed.

(2) The σ between two vowels becomes *h*: ἐνίκαhε (= ἐνίκασε = ἐνίκησε), ἐν hεβόhαις, hίπποις (= ἐν ἡβώσαις ἵπποις), γερωhία = γερουσία. This phenomenon also is due to the old inhabitants of Laconia. It is not found in the Laconian colonies (Tarentum, Thera).[1]

(3) Before a consonant κατά and περί become κατ and περ. The τ is assimilated to the following consonant: Ζεὺς καβάτα = Z. κατβάτα and Z. καβάτα = Z. καταβάτα (= the lightning); Περκλείδας = Περικλείδας, Περφίλας = Περιφίλας. This phenomenon is also Æolic.

---

[1] Cf. Kretschmer in *Nordens Einleitung in die Altertums-wissenschaft*, i, 532.

The later Laconian (the beginning of the 4th century before Christ):

(1) θ passes to σ: σιῶν = θεῶν, σύματος = θύματος, ἀνέσηκε = ἀνέθηκε.

(2) The final ς becomes ρ: ἱερεύρ = ἱερεύς, νεικάλαρ = νικάσας = νικήσας, σιόρ = θεός, βίhωρ = Fίσως, βασιλέαρ = βασιλέας, ἡμέρ [1] = ἡμεῖς.

(3) The dative plural of the third declension has the ending οις, as in North-western dialects: πλειόνοις = *πλείονσι = πλείουσι; Ἀμυκλαιέοις = Ἀμυκλαιεῦσι.

For the accentuation of Doric words we have the authority of old grammarians. They have been collected by Ahrens (*De dialecto dorica,* ii, 26) and by R. Meister (*Bemerkungen zur dorischen Akzentuation,* Leipzig, 1883). The principal rule was that the accent shifted by one unity of quantity (a *mora*) towards the ending of a word. In this manner the words of one syllable perispomena became in Doric oxytona: γλαῦξ became γλαύξ (γλαύ-αυξ ‖ γλαυ-αύξ), σκῶρ σκώρ (σκώ-ωρ ‖ σκω-ώρ); the paroxytona with a long syllable in the ending became perispomena: ἄλλων, ἀλλῶν παίδων, παιδῶν; properispomena and proparoxytona became paroxytona: αἶγες—αῖγες, γυναῖκες—γυναίκες, ἔλεγον—ἐλέγον, ἄγγελοι—ἀγγέλοι, ἄνθρωποι—ἀνθρώποι. But we cannot attribute much value to this evidence, because the grammarians often contradict one another.

[1] In Old-Laconian: ἄμμες.

III. The North-western Group

In general the dialects of this group are akin to the Dorian, but they show the following differences:

Phonetics

(1) The long *ē* and *ō* resulting from contraction appear as εἰ and ου, not as η and ω. This we perceive also in Doric, but only very late.

(2) θ becomes τ or vice versa: χρῆσται = χρῆσθαι, ἐγένονθο = ἐγένοντο.

(3) In the middle gender (genus medium) of the verbs on εω-εο is contracted to ει, not to ου: ποιεῖνται = ποιοῦνται, ἐκκαλείμενος = ἐκκαλούμενος.

(4) ε before ρ becomes α: φάρω = φέρω, Λοκροὶ τοὶ Ϝεσπάριοι = Λ. οἱ ἑσπέριοι, ἀμάρα = ἡμέρα, πατάρα = πατέρα.

Morphology

(1) The dative of the O-stems has the ending οι: ἔδοξε τοῖ κοινοῖ (= τῷ κοινῷ), ἐν Ἀπείροι = ἐν Ἀπείρῳ. But we meet also the ending ωι.

(2) The dative plural of the third declension has the ending οις: ἄνδροις (= ἀνδράσι), ἀγώνοις (= ἀγῶσι), σωμάτοις (= σώμασι).

(3) The ι of the I-stems is present in all the cases: πόλιος (= πόληος = πόλεως), πρυτάνιες (= πρυτάνεις, from πρῶτος).

(4) Instead of the preposition εις with the

accusative answering to the question whither, the preposition ἐν with the accusative was used: ἐν τὰν πόλιν = εἰς τὴν πόλιν.

IV. The Ionic Group

Here we must distinguish between the Old-Ionic dialect, which we know from the poems of Homer and in general from the Greek epic poems, and the later Ionic of the inscriptions and the later authors, as for instance Herodot. Further, the later Ionic must be divided into three sub-divisions: (1) Euboea.—Here the principal features are that ρσ becomes ρρ: θάρρος (= θάρσος); that εννn from ενϝ becomes ε, not ει: ξένος (not ξεῖνος, from ξένϝος). The Euboean dialect is nearly identical with the Attic; but the σ in the endings of words changes to ρ (the rhotacism). In Eretria on Euboea also internal σ becomes ρ: παιρίν = παισίν. (2) The Cyclades.—Here the digamma was preserved longest. (3) Asia Minor.—Here we observe psilosis as in Lesbian: ὅκου = ὅπου. Further, the velar is preserved before a dark vowel: ὅκως, ὅκου, ὁκόσος, ὁκοῖος = ὅπως, ὅπου, ὁπόσος, ὁποῖος.

Phonetics

Long ā became a sound like the a in 'fate'. This sound is indicated by the letter H. Originally this letter indicated an aspirate and it is well known that it has preserved this use in Latin. As in the Ionic of Asia Minor, the spiritus asper disappeared and the name of the letter was *'etha*, not *hetha*, as before. The pronunciation of the letter was now not *h*, but " *ae* "—a sound between *e* and *a*.

In some cases also a short a became η: ἀληθείη (= the Attic ἀλήθεια), ἀτελείη (= ἀτέλεια).

Very early we find in Ionic the propensity to contract neighbouring vowels to one sound[1]: a + o became an ω (ἐνίκων from *ἐνίκαον, Ἀγλωσθένης from Ἀγλαοσθένης). In ε + o the sound o was a back sound, for in writing it was expressed by υ (= *u* in ' bull '): πλεῦνες instead of πλέονες, Κλεύμαχος instead of Κλεόμαχος, ἐξαιρεύμεθα instead of ἐξαιρεόμεθα. After vowels ε + o became simply U (= ου) and the ε was assimilated to o: εο—οο—ου. Further, ε + ω became ω and ε + a—a. In the dialect of Homer we find a preparatory step towards the contraction of ε + o and ε + ω ; ε becomes a consonant *j*: φιλέομεν sounds as φιλjόμεν, Πηληιάδεω as Πηληιάδjω. Further, ε + η becomes in Ionic η : Ἀριστοκλῆς =Ἀριστοκλέης ; o + ε and o + o = ου.

The digamma, which was preserved a long time in Æolic and also in Doric, disappeared very early in Ionic. Already in the 7th century before Christ, Archilochus writes μετ' ἀστῶν instead of μετὰ Ϝαστῶν, πολλ' οἶδε instead of πολλὰ Ϝοῖδε,

---

[1] In the epic dialect the contraction is not yet developed, and in general we observe in Ionian only the propensity to contraction. It is fully developed in Attic. Cf. Bechtel, *Die Vocalcontraction bei Homer*, Halle, 1908.

although in the Cyclades (Archilochus was born on Paros, one of the Cyclades) the digamma was longest heard, as is proved by the inscriptions.

If after a liquid or a nasal the digamma or a sibilant disappeared, the so-called compensatory lengthening ensued in Ionic with the exception of Attic and Eubœan, that is the preceding vowel was drawled or pronounced darkly: ξεῖνος (pronounce: *ksēnos*; instead of *ξένϜος), κούρη (*kurē*; from *κόρϜη),[1] δούρατα (from δορϜατα. Cf. the Slavonic *dŭrvo* and the Russian *dérevo* = wood, but also = tree), εἶναι (*ēnai*) from *ἔσ-ναι (cf. the Latin *es-se*).

The guttural *q* has been preserved in the Ionic of Asia Minor before dark vowels, whilst elsewhere it became a π.

The double sigma caused by assimilation became in Ionic sometimes a simple sigma: ὄσσος (from *ὄτjος) became ὄσος.

A long vowel and a short one exchanged their quantity: the quantitatory metathesis; Χρὴ ὄν became Χρεών, Θρεΐκιος—Θρηΐκιος, Πυθαγόρηο—Πυθαγόρεω. If both of two neighbouring vowels were long, the first was shortened: the ending αων became εων, ἤως—ἔως. Sometimes the second vowel, which became long by metathesis, was shortened: βασιλέος instead of βασιλέως (from βασιλῆϜος) by analogy with the genitives on ος. Likewise Χρεόν by analogy with ἐξόν, etc.

---

[1] Cf. in Russian: *Kúrva* = a strumpet.

Morphology

The *A*- and *O*-stems had until the 4th century before Christ the endings αισι and οισι in the dative plural, but also αις and οις.[1] From the third century these latter were exclusively used. Sometimes the α in αισι became an η (as in Ionic). The endings ησι and ης are first found in Homer. In inscriptions we find τῆις συνθήκηις.

Alongside of the regular declension of the I-stems we find a declension with the stem η : πόλις, genitive : πόλιος or πόληος (in Attic with metathesis : πόλεως). This η-stem originated under the influence of the *ē* ending of the old locative. The form of the locative was at first *πολι-η, then *πολjη (cf. the Slavonian form *Kyjevē* = at Kiev), and finally *πολη. This form was taken as a stem, from which the genitive πόλη-ος was formed. Before dark vowels η was shortened and later also before open ones. Thus appeared the forms πόλεος, πόλεες, πόλεσι instead of πόληος, etc.

The first and second persons of the plural personal pronoun are in Ionic ἡμεῖς and ὑμεῖς. But in primitive Greek the forms were ἄμμες and ὔμμες (cf. in Sanscrit the accusative *asmān* and *yuṣmān*, the nominative *vayam* and *yūyam*). The genitive was ἀμμέων and ὑμμέων, as in the εσ-stems. The nominative plural of these stems had

---

[1] Homer uses αισι and οισι as endings of substantives and αις and οις as endings of the article : τοῖς and ταῖς.

in Ionic the ending εις: *εὐγενέσες, εὐγενέες, εὐγενεῖς by contraction. Thus by analogy appeared the forms *ἄμμεις and ὔμμεις and later ἡμεῖς and ὑμεῖς (Ionic η instead of α, spiritus asper by analogy with the second person, and the double consonant made simple like ὅσος instead of ὅσσος).

Instead of the accusative αὐτόν and the dative αὐτῷ, αὐτός replacing, as well known, in Greek the primitive third person of the personal pronoun; stem: σϝε preserved in the form of the reflexive pronoun σϝεαυτόν-ἑαυτίν, we find in the epic dialect and in the elder Ionic μιν.

The ending of the infinitive of the thematic conjugation is in Ionic ειν from *εσεν-εεν (*φερεσεν, *φέρεεν, φέρειν). Cf. the Latin ending ere from *ese (as in es-se).

The infinitive of the athematic conjugation has in Ionic besides the ending εναι from ϝεναι (cf. the Sanscrit da-vane), sometimes also the ending ναι. That has come about in the following manner: if the ending of the stem of a verb was η, this η contracted with the ε of the ending εναι: *βη-ένα became βῆναι. Later the ending ναι was taken as the ending of the infinitive: φάναι, δεικνύ-ναι. Also already in Ionic we observe that the athematic conjugation had become thematic: δεικνύει, διδοῦν = διδόναι (from *διδόϝεν *διδόεν), καθιστᾶν (from *καθ-ιστα-ϝεν), τιθεῖ (= τίθησι), etc. In modern Greek the athematic conjugation has completely disappeared.

The third person imperfect singular of εἶναι (from *εσ-ναι) was originally ἦς (= in Sanscrit *as*). In Ionic we find ἦν formed on the analogy of the plural: in Sanscrit *āsan*; in Latin *erant*—the *t* on the analogy of *sun-t*. In Ionic first *ἦσεν appeared, then ἦεν (in Homer), and finally ἦν. That the form of the plural became the form of the singular is due to the general resemblance of the ending of the third person singular of the imperfect: ε. The same resemblance brought also the addition to this ε of a ν, which in ἦεν was organic. That this ν was not organic in the conjugation of the verbs in general, is deduced from the fact that it was often omitted. It is usually called ν ἐφελκυστικόν: ἔφερε and ἔφερεν were both in use. The well-known rule, that ν ἐφελκυστικόν is to be added before vowels, was formulated by the grammarians of Alexandria. Later it was added also to the endings τι and σι.

Instead of the Æolic particle κε and the Doric κα we meet in Ionic ἄν. Originally this particle marked a question, and in Latin it has preserved this use. In Greek the particle indicates a possibility. The German *wohl*, which expresses both a possibility and a question, may be compared: *wird er wohl kommen?* and *er wird wohl kommen*. In modern Greek, where ἄν, κε, and κα have all disappeared, their place is taken by θά. For the origin of this particle see below (p. 131).

As among the Dorian dialects the Laconian had

its remarkable peculiarities, so among the Ionic
dialects the Attic deserves special consideration.
That it belonged to the Ionic group is shown by
the fact that in Attic also α changes to η. There
are also other phenomena common to Attic and
Ionic: ἡμεῖς, the ν ἐφελκυστικόν, the particle ἄν, οἱ
not τοι, ἔθεσαν, ἔδοσαν, ἐλύθησαν instead of ἔθεν,
etc., ὅπου instead of ὅπει.

Phonetics of Attic

In the diphthongs ει, αι, and οι the first vowel
was prominent and has in some words ousted the
second: ἱέρε(ι)α, ᾽Ακαδήμεα, ᾽Αθήναα (= ᾽Αθηναια),
ποέω (contracted to ποιῶ).

After ρ and thin vowels ε, ι, and υ[1] the pure
sound α was preserved in contrast to the Ionic η.
This is the so-called α purum, which originated
from the analogy of forms like ὑγιᾶ (ὑγιέα) or
ἐνδεᾶ.[2] Kretschmer explains this phenomenon by a
dissimilation. But the influence of ρ ceased in
later times. Therefore, besides ὑγιᾶ from ὑγιέα we
have τριήρη (not *τριήρα) from τριήρεα. It must
also be observed that originally the α purum seems
not to have existed at all. In the Attic of Æschylus
we have πρῆγμα instead of πρᾶγμα.

Instead of ρσ we have in the later Attic after the
Peloponnesian War ρρ (θαρρεῖν instead of θαρσεῖν,

---

[1] In Attic υ was pronounced very early as *u* in French
words (*lune*). In modern Greek υ is pronounced as *i*.
[2] Except after ι and ε, εα was contracted to η.

ἄρρην instead of ἄρσην) and instead of σσ—ττ (μέλιττα instead of μέλισσα). We find the latter phenomenon also in North-west Greek.

The Ionic diphthong ηι, which arose from αι, becomes in Attic ει. In Ionic, κληίς from *κλαϜις— cf. the Latin clavis; in Attic, κλείς; in Ionic, ληιτουργίη from λαός, ληός; in Attic, λειτουργία; in Ionic, κρύπτῃ; in later Attic, κρύπτει as second person of the passive present. In Attic inscriptions of later time we read ἔδοξε τεῖ βουλεῖ instead of τῇ βουλῇ. Also the simple η becomes in later Attic ει: ἤδειμεν = ἤδημεν; βασιλεῖς = βασιλῆς.

Morphology of Attic

The genitive of the masculine-stems in A has the same ending as the O-stems: ου-πολίτου from πολίτης (η here from α). This is due to the analogy of the ending of the genitive plural ων, which is common to both stems.

The nominative plural of substantives in ευς had till the middle of the 4th century before Christ the ending ῆς; later the ending εις appears.

The forms of the personal pronoun of the third person, σφᾶς (from σφέας), σφίσιν, σφῶν, about 400 before Christ became obsolete in Attic and were superseded by the forms of the reflexive pronoun: ἑαυτῶν, ἑαυτοῖς, ἑαυτούς from *σφε-αυτῶν, etc.).

The elder form ξύν after the Peloponnesian War gave way to σύν.

Instead of οὐδείς appears οὐθείς.

The forms of the third person of the Perfect and Plusquam perfect passive plural were supplied by a periphrasis with the participle passive and the present and the imperfect of the verb εἶναι. Instead of τετάχαται (primitive form: *τεταγνται from τάσσω) we find in Attic τεταγμένοι or τεταγμέναι εἰσίν, and instead of ἐτετάχατο—τεταγμένοι ἦσαν. In the vulgar Attic also periphrases with the present participle active occur (Aristophanes, *Ranae*, 26, βαδίζων εἰμί instead of βαδίζω ; *Thesmophoriazusae*, 77, ἔστ᾽ ἔτι ζῶν instead of ἔτι ζῇ).

The Vulgar Attic

Because of its relatively early development, the literary language in Attica very soon obtained a fixed form. Not so the living language of everyday use. We know that it was always changing. This is proved by the inscriptions which deal with private life ; for example, the inscriptions on vases [1] and the tablets of execration.[2] Another source of our knowledge of the ordinary language in Attica in the 5th, the 4th, and the 3rd centuries before Christ is the free and natural language of the comedies.[3]

The study of vulgar Attic is very important, for from this dialect, the so-called κοινή being an

[1] Cf. P. Kretschmer, *Die griechischen Vaseninschriften*, Gütersloh, 1894.
[2] W. Rabehl, *De sermone defixionum atticarum*, Berlin, 1906.
[3] O. Lottich, *De sermone vulgari Atticorum ex Aristophanis fabulis cognoscendo*, Halle, 1908 ; G. Setti in *Museo Italiano*, i, 113.

intermediation, the modern Greek has originated. We find here, for instance, substantives with the ending ι(ον), but without the diminutive force, which such substantives generally had in ancient Greek. Already in the lines of Aristophanes, δύο λυχνίδια does not signify ' two little lamps ', but simply ' two lamps ', as in modern Greek.[1] Further, in consequence of the continual inter-course between Attica and the other regions of the Greek world, words of foreign dialects pene-trated into Attic. Such words ousted the original expressions and continue their life in modern Greek.[2] For instance, we find in the vulgar Attic the word βουνός, which belonged to the dialect of Cyrene, and we find it again in the modern Greek word βουνό—mountain (instead of the old word ὄρος). The characteristic features of the vulgar Attic are the following.

Phonetics

We perceive that already the feeling for the quantity of the vowels (if long, or short) is weakened. Likewise, the inclination to the so-called itacism is undeniable (the pronunciation of η and ει as i in ' pin '). Already in the 5th century before Christ, we find orthographical confusion: η with ε, ο

---

[1] This was common already in the 1st century of our era. In the seventh tale of Dio Chrysostom we find the following words on ιον, *which are not diminutives:* βοΐδιον, μοσχάριον, σιτάριον, φασκώλιον, χιτώνιον, σελήνιον (!), λινάριον, οἰνάριον.

[2] Cf. Ps. Xenophon, Ἀθηναίων πολιτεία: ἔπειτα φωνήν πᾶσαν ἀκούοντες ἐξελέξαντο (οἱ Ἀθηναῖοι) τοῦτο μὲν ἐκ τῆς, τοῦτο δὲ ἐκ τῆς.

with ω, ει with ι or with ε (Μείμνον instead of
Μέμνων). Instead of ἐμοί was written ἠμοί, με
instead of μη, ις instead of εις, συμφέριν instead
of συμφέρειν. Vowels were assimilated in adjacent
syllables: Τριπτόλομος instead of Τριπτόλεμος.
Thence came the later false spelling of the name
of the dynasty of Ptolemaios: Πτολομαῖοι.

Between consonants a vowel was inserted under
the influence of the following or preceding one:
Ηερεμες = Ἑρμῆς, Ἐπιδόρομος = Ἐπίδρομος. On
the other side vowels between consonants are
ousted: Ἀθένεθν = Ἀθήνηθεν, ἐποίεσν = ἐποίησεν.

The nasals are suppressed before consonants:
Ἀταλάτε = Ἀταλάντη, τὴ Πασιφάνου = τὴν Πασι-
φανου. In modern Greek this is very common:
ἄτρωπος = ἄνθρωπος.

In the vulgar Attic we remark a predilection
for the aspirate: ηελπίδα = ἐλπίδα, Θέθις = Θέτις,
θροφός = τροφός, Χόλχος = Κόλχος. But instead of
σθ we find στ: βόλεστε = βούλεσθε.

Instead of δ we find σ: Ἄσμητος = Ἄδμητος.
But before vowels δ becomes λ: Ὀλυττές =
Ὀδυσσεύς.[1]

Morphology

Instead of ευς we find the ending ής (ές) or ύς:
Προμεθές, Θεσύς.

Instead of παῖς, we have παῦς (perhaps on the
analogy of γραῦς) or πᾶς.

[1] Cf. the Latin form of the name: Ulysses.

Instead of πίε, we read on vases πίει (χαῖρε καὶ πίει). Hirt explains the ι here as a particle; cf. ἴ-θι, ἴσ-θι. Perhaps it is a contamination of the forms πίε and πίθι.

Instead of ἀνάβηθι and κατάβηθι, we find ἀνάβα and κατάβα.

Chapter IV

THE Κοινή

From the 4th century before Christ we remark in the inscriptions the gradual disappearance of the numerous old local dialects. The small Greek cities were stepping out of their secluded life. In the great kingdoms of the Diadochi, where Greeks of all tribes met, there was a necessity of a common official language understood by all Greeks. The old dialects, especially those in which no significant literature had existed, became little by little obsolete. Already in the 4th century before Christ at Argos the old conjunction αἰ gave way to the conjunction εἰ. In the same century in Crete βούλομαι took the place of the old verbs λῶ (λῆς, etc.) and δείλομαι. In the 3rd century πόλεος and πόλεως appear in this island instead of πόλιος, and in the 2nd century εἶναι instead of ἦμεν. Mixed forms also are found: in Bœotia ἅως instead of the old ᾶς is a form due to the Attic ἕως. Likewise in the κοινή διάλεκτος of the Ætolian league we meet εἴκα instead of the pure form αἴκα. In the 1st and 2nd centuries of our era, Strabo and Pausanias tell us that it was an exception that in Messenia and in Rhodos they still understood the old Doric dialect. It is true that even in the 3rd

century of our era we meet with inscriptions in
the old dialects, but this was an affectation of the
same kind as the artificial resuscitation of the old
Attic dialect in the 1st and 2nd century of our
era by some authors, as Plutarch and Lucian (the
so-called Atticism). That the old dialects had
ceased to exist in the living language of the time,
we may infer from blunders, as, for instance,
ἀμετάβλατον instead of ἀμετάβλητον. The writer
clearly intended to form a Dorism by substituting
α for η. He did not know that in this case the
η (= ē) was inherited from the primitive language.
On the other side, we read in an inscription of
Byzantium of the 1st century the purely Ionic
form ἡγήσατο instead of the Doric ἀγήσατο, although
this city was originally Doric. In general it may be
said that from the 1st century of our era the
Dorisms in the inscriptions of the old Doric cities
go no further than the substitution of α for η.
The intention was to give the documents a vener-
able appearance.

In private correspondence just as much as in
official documents and in the literature generally
(here until the Atticism) the old dialects gave way
to the κοινὴ διάλεκτος. Scholars have produced
formerly very different opinions on the character
of this language. Niebuhr thought that it was the
language of the common people. Clark believed
it to be a lingua franca, Ducange—a much corrupted
language (lingua corruptissima), Lobeck—a mixture

F

of all the dialects (omnium dialectorum commune
deversorium). At present the κοινή is regarded as
the result of the development of the Greek language
from about the year 300 before Christ. As to the
composition of the κοινή scholars have not yet
agreed. Sturz (in *De dialecto alexandrina*) like Lobeck
believed it to be a mixture of several dialects:
Attic, Macedonian, and others. Among our con-
temporaries Kretschmer in *Wiener Sitzungsberichte*,
Band 143 (1900), agreed with him. Kretschmer
thinks that the κοινή borrowed from Bœotian the
change of αι to ε, of οι to υ and ι, from North-west
Greek the forms τοῖς ἄνδροις and τοὺς λέγοντες, from
Dorian—υ instead of β and the forms τόλμα (instead
of τόλμη) and θέρμα (= θέρμη ; cf. *Herodian*, i,
255). With Ionian the κοινή participated the loss
of the spiritus asper, the non-contracted forms
ὀστέα, ἀνθέων and σσ and ρς instead of the Attic
ττ and ρρ. But another contemporary—Brugmann
—declared that the κοινή is a development only
of one dialect, namely, the Macedonian. It is now
generally believed that the κοινή is descended from
the old Attic. This is the opinion of Hatzidakis and
Krumbacher. In Antiquity already we have the
testimony of Eirenaios in his work περὶ τῆς
Ἀλεξανδρέων διαλέκτου, ὅτι ἔστιν ἐκ τῆς Ἀτθίδος.
But A. Thumb supposes also a strong Ionic
influence and this may be perceived already in the
works of Aristoteles and even of Xenophon (cf.
Moulton, *Einleitung in die Sprache des Neuen*

THE κοινή 83

Testaments, 1911, p. 45). We meet non-contracted forms (ὀρέων, χειλέων), Ionic forms in general: χέρσος instead of χέρρος, πράσσω (= πράττω in Attic), οὐδείς (= οὐθείς in Attic), λαός (= λεώς in Attic), βασίλισσα (=βασίλεια), and psilosis; assimilation, where it is not allowed in Attic: ἔννατος (from *ἐ-νέϜατος; in Attic—ἔνατος). Nevertheless, W. Schmid has denied this influence (*Goettinger Gelehrtenanzeiger*, 1895, 34).[1]

In relation to Attic, the influence of the vulgar Attic on the κοινή is indisputable (θροφός, γίνομαι = γίγνομαι, ἀνάβα, and κατάβα). We also remark a peculiarity, which is generally observed in the development of languages, as for example in the transition of Latin into the Roman languages. A word already obsolete in the literary style, and continuing to live only in the slang or occasionally appearing in the poetic style, suddenly regains its full civil rights, as for example, *caballus* instead of the usual Latin word *equus*, appears in the Italian *cavallo* and in the French *cheval*. In the same manner we meet a great number of old obsolete words revived in the κοινή.

We may be sure that it has developed out of the Attic, what is very natural, this dialect having been the language of cultivated Greeks ever since the 5th century before Christ; on the other side it

[1] But even in Modern Greek traces of the old Ionic might be pointed at: ἄκρη = ἄκρα, βάθρακας = βάτραχος (cf. κιθών = χιθών), φερνή = προίξ, βασίλισσα, οὖλος = ὅλος (in Cyprus, Crete, Chios, the western coast).

cannot be denied that in the κοινή many non-Attic elements are to be found. Beside Ionic words and forms we find also Macedonian (ῥύμη, παρεμβολή) and even Dorian words and forms: ξεναγός, μαρυκῶμαι, μάκων, the forms of the aorist on ξα instead of σα: ἐχώριξα. Many non-Greek elements also have found their way into the κοινή. Here not only the vocabulary is concerned; the phonetics of the language were still more deeply affected. We observe in the inscriptions of Asia Minor and in the papyri found in Egypt that the mediæ, the tenues, and the aspiratæ are often confused. Instead of τ we meet δ (ἀποδισάτω = ἀποτεισάτω, δέκτων = τέκτων) and vice versa: δέτωκας = δεδωκας. This is a consequence of the contact with foreign neighbouring nations. In the language of the Copts, which descends from the ancient Egyptian, we find just this peculiarity. In the same manner we can see why the vulgar κοινή confounds I (the English i in ' pin ') and E (the English e in ' let '): γίγονις, γέγονες, ἀναγενώσκοντες = ἀναγινώσκοντες. The sound υ appears sometimes as ι, sometimes as ε: σίμβιος = σύμβιος, γενή = γυνή, ἐπέρ = ὑπέρ, θυράπων = θεράπων. Here especially the influence of Phrygian is to be discerned.

Besides this influence from the languages lying to the east of the Greeks, it would be natural to expect some influence from Latin as a consequence of the intimate relations of the Greeks and the

Romans from the 3rd century before Christ, and
of the circumstance that Latin was until the 7th
century the official language of the Greek East.[1]
In grammar, however, this influence appears very
weak. Latinisms might be expected in the works
of Romans writing Greek. But even here some
phenomena, which might be explained as Latinisms,
seem to be an organic development of the κοινή
itself; for instance, the omission of the article, the
periphrastic conjugation, the historical perfect
instead of the aorist. On the other side the endings
ις and ιν instead of ιος and ιον must be regarded as
genuine Latinisms. Following the type of Latin
words like *familiaris* or *augustalis* genuine Greek
words changed their ending: κύρις instead of
κύριος. Further, Latin idioms passed into Greek by
literal translation: ἐνεύχομαι = *imprecor* (in the
New Testament), ὑπ᾽ ἐξουσίαν ἄγειν = *in potestatem
redigere* (in Polybios), ἐργασίαν διδόναι = *operam dare*,
ἠόνα ξύρειν = *oram radere*. According to the Latin
idiom ὅς (= *qui*) was sometimes followed by the
subjunctive, if it had the signification of ὥστε:
οὐδὲ ἀπόκρυφον (ἐστι), ὃ οὐ γνωσθήσεται καὶ
εἰς φανερὰν ἔλθῃ (*Evangelium Lucæ*, 8, 17). Finally
it may be mentioned that the Latin ending *anus*
is very often observed in the κοινή: Χριστιανός,
Ἡροδιανός.[2]

[1] Cf. A. Budinszky, *Ausbreitung d. lat. Sprache*, Berlin, 1881.
[2] The ending ατος (= in Latin: *atus : amatus*) is due to
Italian influence in the Middle Ages: εἶναι φευγάτος = *e fuggito*;
ἔχω πεμπάτο = *ho mandato*. We meet μαντάτο in the ballad of
Armuris.

More important than the grammatical influence of Latin on the κοινή was the influence of the Latin vocabulary. The lexicographer Hesychius mentions a great number of Latin words in Greek: φίσκος, κόμης, ῥέδα *rhaeda* (properly a Celtic word, which passed into Latin), κάβαλλος, κερβησία (*cerevisia*), κουμέρκιον, μαγκίπιον, λουκάνικον, πέρνα. Further, we meet many Latin words in the text of the New Testament: κουστωδία, μάκελλον, μόδιος. The Latin influence may be observed also in the works of the Greeks of the Middle Ages. In the poem on the conquest of Constantinople by the Turks we meet the verb ἀκραριεύω, which is identical with ἀγραριεύω in Hesychius and with the Latin (*per*) *agrare*. Then we meet the Latin words κηνσεύω, κήνσευσις, πάκτον (= *pactum*). At that time even ancient Greek words were sometimes explained by means of Latin: χειρόμακτρον was explained by the Latin μανδήλιον (*mandelium*), πέταυρα by τίγναι. In modern Greek, Latin words have sometimes ousted the genuine Greek ones; we have κόκινος (*coccinus* = 'scarlet') instead of ἐρυθρός. Many such words seem to have been adopted at a very early period. For instance, τὸ σπίτι (= οἰκία, from *hospitium*) was adopted, when *ti* in Latin was not yet pronounced as *zi*, i.e. before the 6th century of our era.[1]

The study of the grammatical structure of the κοινή is more difficult than that of the local dialects.

[1] Cf. L. Lafoscade, ' Influence du Latin sur le Grec ' in J. Psichari, *Études de philologie neogrecque*, ii, Paris, 1892.

This seems a paradox, for this form of the language has existed more than a thousand years. We might expect a copious quantity of literary monuments to afford us the possibility of studying this dialect. But this is not so. In literature the κοινή in its genuine form appears very rarely. Authors wished to employ a loftier style and despised the κοινή as a language of common daily use. As we have already had occasion to observe, since the 1st century of our era authors wrote almost exclusively in old Attic, a dialect sanctified by the names of renowned writers. An exception were the books of the mathematicians, the surgeons, and the philosophers belonging to the sect of Pythagoras. The surgeons nevertheless wrote rather in the old Ionic, following the tradition of the celebrated Hippocrates; the Neo-Pythagoreans in memory of Philolaus, who for the first time wrote down the maxims of Pythagoras, used to write in Doric (Philolaus was a Dorian born at Tarentum, a Dorian colony). As to the documents and private letters found in great quantity in Egypt, many are written by uneducated men, who were often not of Greek origin. Their barbarisms and orthographical blunders render the study of the genuine language of the period very difficult.

The most important and the most copious source for the study of the κοινή, beside such historians as Polybius and Diodorus, is the Holy Scripture, i.e. the Greek of the New Testament and the Greek translation of the Old (the Septuaginta). Of the New Testament a part was written in Greek from the very beginning, Greek being at that time the language of the widest currency. In these writings we find indeed the genuine Greek language used in the first centuries of our era. This may be proved by the fact that the old school-rhetorists spoke of this dialect as being vulgar. Many even called it barbarous and full of solœcisms, i.e. of non-Greek expressions; for example, hebraisms. In the 17th century a quarrel began between the so-called Hebraists and Purists. The former even declared that the text of the Greek New Testament was a literal translation from the Hebrew. They said, for example, that ἔσονται εἰς σάρκα μίαν is a Hebraism. But a genuine Greek expression found already in Theognis (6th century before Christ) may be compared: τὸ κακὸν δοκέον γίγνεσθαι εἰς ἀγαθόν. The Purists, on the contrary, declared the text of the New Testament to be genuine Greek.[1] This debate seems not to be settled yet. Viteau in his *Étude sur le Grec du Nouveau Testament* (1893) found a great admixture of foreign Semitic elements in the Greek of the New Testament, whilst Deissmann in his *Bibelstudien* (1895 and 1897) and his *Licht vom Osten* (1909) declares the language to be a pure κοινή. The existence of some Hebraisms in our text cannot be denied (ὁ κριτὴς

[1] Cf. Wiener-Schmidel, *Grammatik des neutestamentlichen Sprachidioms*, 1894, pp. 4 et seq.

τῆς ἀδικίας, σκεῦος ἐκλογῆς, γλῶσσα = λαός, χεῖλος
= γλῶσσα), but they are relatively few. Still
less important is the influence of Hebrew on the
grammatical structure of the language of the
Greek Bible. It must be observed that in regard
to the language the books of the Holy Scripture
are not uniform; nor is the language proper so
much concerned as the style. St. Luke, for example,
tries to write a pure Greek. He generally avoids
foreign words (Aramaic or Latin) and translates
them into pure Greek. He employs Attic forms.
Instead of the historical perfect κεκάθικεν he uses
the aorist ἐκάθισεν; instead of ἴδιος he employs the
obsolete ἑαυτοῦ; instead of the analogical form
οἴδασι (οἶδα) he says in correct conformity to
the Attic—ἴσασι. Also he uses Attic words instead
of words properly belonging to the κοινή. Instead
of τρώγω he says ἐσθίω, instead of πτῶμα—σῶμα,
instead of διασκορπίζω—σπείρω. In opposition to
the Gospel of St. Luke the Gospel of St. Matthew
contains a relatively large number of Semitisms,
which is very natural, because the text of this
evangelist was originally written in Hebrew (ἑβραΐδι
διαλέκτῳ. Cf. Papias in the *Historia ecclesiastica*
of Eusebius, iii, 39, 16). G. Dalman in his *Worte
Jesu* (i, p. 16) observes especially the following
Semitisms in the text of the New Testament:
ἀφεὶς καταλιπών (= to go off), ἐλθὼν ἐρχόμενος,
βασιλεία τῶν οὐρανῶν, πατὴρ ὁ ἐν τοῖς οὐρανοῖς.
Such expressions we find also in the pagan

mysteries (ἀδελφοί, πατήρ = priest in the mysteries of Mithra).

Some modern scholars (among others A. Thumb) [1] have pointed to yet another important source for the study of the κοινή. The dialects of Modern Greek, as has been mentioned above, have developed out of the κοινή and might help us to draw conclusions on the form of the latter, its vocabulary and also its grammar. But here we meet with a great difficulty. The link between the κοινή and the modern dialects, the so-called vulgar Greek, the language of conversation of the Greeks of the Middle Ages is known to us very imperfectly, because monuments of this language are preserved for us only from a late period. Nevertheless some peculiarities of the κοινή may be linked with those of Modern Greek. We observe, for example, in the inscriptions of this period the disappearance of the sound *i* in syllables preceding others containing this sound: πέρσυ instead of πέρυσυ (the υ sounded already like a pure *i*). The same peculiarity is found in Modern Greek also, namely in the northern dialects, where it has been explained by the influence of the language of the neighbouring Albanian tribes. Perhaps also in the κοινή this peculiarity was confined to certain regions. Further, we find in the Modern Greek the so-called irrational γ (a sound similar to *gh*), as for example in κλαί-

[1] Cf. *Classical Quarterly*, 1914, pp. 181 et seq. : ' On the value of Modern Greek for the study of the κοινή.'

(γ)-ω (= κλαίω), ἀκου-(γ)-ω (= ἀκούω). This sound also does not appear everywhere, but only in certain regions. In others, on the contrary, the genuine γ has disappeared: καταωή (= καταγωγή), μααζίν (= μαγαζίν). This we meet also in ancient Greek (cf. Meineke, *Fragmenta comicor. græcor*, i, 191: ὀλίον ἔλεγεν). The irrational γ can be traced through the vulgar texts till to the κοινή (cf. Krumbacher, ' Ein irrationaler Spirant im Griechischen,' in *Berichte der bayerischen Akademie*, 1893). The following characteristic peculiarities may be also mentioned. In many dialects of southern Greece the guttural *k* before *e* and *i* becomes a palatal *c* or *z*. The conjunction καί is pronounced as the syllable *ce* in Italian (for instance, in the word *cena*). The pronunciation of the Latin *c* in its transition to *z* and the Italian *c* (cf. in Latin, *Kikero—Zizero*; in Italian, *cicerone*) may be compared. A similar change of sound may be observed in the κοινή. The Roman name ' Lucia ' is spelled Λουσία instead of Λουκία. In an inscription of about the year 400 of our era κύκλα is written ζύκλα. The change of λφ to ρφ observed in some regions of southern Greece is also found in the κοινή (ἀδερφός instead of ἀδελφός). Finally, the ending ων instead of ωσι of the third person plural of the subjunctive present and second aorist we meet in many regions of Modern Greece is found, for example, in a papyrus of the year 148 of our era: ἀγάγων = ἀγάγωσι.

Although the κοινή was early split into many
dialects (the ancestors of the modern Greek
dialects), it was not called a common language for
nothing; it had its own peculiarities, by which it
was distinguished from the vulgar dialects, and it
lay above them all, as the modern German literary
language lies above all the numerous dialects of
German. If we now ask: what was the general
character of the κοινή ?—the best answer is given
by the German scholar Robert Helbing in his
Grammar of the Septuagint : in the language of the
κοινή-period the general tendency is towards
simplification. We may add, towards *regularity*.
Already in the phonetics this tendency is manifest :
diphthongs are exchanged for simple vowels :
κατεσκέασε instead of κατεσκεύασε ; κυριέουσα instead
of κυριεύουσα. Many substantives of the third
declension inflected irregularly are now inflected
regularly according to the second declension or
have been ousted by others of the second declension
and become obsolete. The forms ἄρνα, ἀρνός, etc.,
are replaced by ἀρνίον, ἀρνίου, etc., or ἀμνόν, ἀμνοῦ ;
instead of ὄρνις, ὄρνιθος, etc., in the κοινή-period
ὄρνεον, ὀρνέου, etc., was used, or πετεινόν (cf. in
Modern Greek: πτηνό—(ν) or πουλί—a Roman
word ; in Italian *pollo*, in French *poule*). Instead
of the irregular ναῦς we find πλοῖον. Already from
the 4th century before Christ the word υἱός was
declined according to the second declension :
υἱός, υἱοῦ, etc., not υἱέος, υἱεῖ, etc. The particle ἄν

disappears (Moulton, *Gr. N.T.*, p. 192). Some forms
of the verbal inflection have totally disappeared
in the κοινή: the dual is replaced by the plural [1]
and the optative by the subjunctive. Instead of two
aorists we find only one. In the active the first
aorist ousted the second, and in the passive—vice
versa. The second aorist is sometimes replaced by
the first or alters its ending ον to α (εἶπα instead of
εἶπον) and in the middle—όμην to άμην (ἐπεβαλάμην,
ἐγενάμην).[2] In modern Greek only twelve second
aorists still exist. The syllabic augment is rejected,
but the temporal augment appears also in the
infinitive and in the subjunctive: ἀνηλῶσι instead
of ἀναλῶσι. If forms of a verb were formed from
different stems only one was preserved. This
tendency we observe very early. Already Epichar-
mus formed the perfect πέποσχα (from πάσχω)
instead of πέπονθα. The aorist of the liquid verb
is formed like the aorist of the verbs with the stem
in ε: ἐνέμησα (= ἔνειμα), ἐγάμησα (= ἔγημα). The
perfect has lost its peculiar meaning (continuance
of a past action in the present) and becoming
superfluous is ousted by the aorist. In the cases
when it appears in Modern Greek it has the same
value with the aorist: ἄκουκα = ἤκουσα, ἐκάθικα
(= κεκάθικα) = ἐκάθισα.

---

[1] Cf. Hermann Schmid, ' De duali Græcorum et emoriente
et reviviscente,' *Breslauer Phil. Abhandlungen*, iv, 6 (1893). We
find here the bibliography of the question.

[2] In modern Greek ἔγινα. Mediating forms were : ἐλάβοσαν,
εἶπασαν, παρεκάλουσαν.

The characteristic tendency in the κοινή towards simplification had also an influence on the pronunciation of Greek sounds.[1] But although the pronunciation was changed, the orthography was preserved and we are made aware of this change chiefly by orthographical blunders in the inscriptions and papyri: ι, ει, η, ῃ, υ, and οι are often confused, for by degrees the pronunciation of all these orthographical signs was becoming the same: ι. Also the transcriptions of Greek in foreign alphabets are for us an important source of information. From transcriptions into Hebrew, for example, we know that about the beginning of our era the spiritus asper had ceased to be heard [2]: ὑποθήκη is spelt *ipothiki*, ἕδρα—*edra*. In Coptic texts we find it sometimes on a wrong place: *helpizein* instead of *elpizein*, *hethnos* instead of *ethnos*. Similarly in Hebrew texts: *chakra* instead of *akra*, and in Syriac *hepi* = ἐπί. The latter peculiarity we find also in Greek texts: ἀφελπίζοντες = ἀπελπίζοντες, οὐχ ὀλίγος = οὐκ ὀλίγος. From this we may infer that the complete disappearance of the spiritus asper was preceded by a period in which its use was uncertain and fluctuating; it

---

[1] Cf. Blass, *Die Aussprache des Griechischen* [3], 1888 ; E. H. Sturtevant, *The Pronunciation of Greek and Latin*, Chicago, 1920.

[2] In the 3rd century before Christ the spiritus was still audible. In the papyrus of Herodas we read οὐδὲ εἷς and οὐδὲ ἕν instead of οὐδείς and οὐδέν. Aristotle expressly distinguished the pronunciation of ὅρος and ὄρος, although these words were in his time written alike : ΟΡΟΣ (Cf. Σοφιστ. ἔλεγχ. 177β, 3 : ἐν γεγραμμένοις ταὐτὸν ὄνομα, τὰ δὲ φθεγγόμενα οὐ ταὐτά.)

was this uncertainty that caused the invention of special signs to mark the spiritus.

The Morphology of the κοινή

The vocative is no longer distinguished from the nominative. Nor is there any longer a difference in the declension of substantives in α purum and those in α impurum: μάχαιρα, μαχαίρης, μαχαίρη, etc. The genitive of the A-system ends in η[1] (analogy with Ἑρμῆ and πολίτα(ο)).

The endings ιων and ιστος of the adjectives have lost their comparative and superlative meaning; they were taken as of the positive, and therefore from μείζων (= *μεγ-ιων) as a positive the comparative μειζώτερος was formed and from μέγιστος —μεγιστότερος. In the Epistle to the Ephesians of St. Paul (iii, 8) we find the form ἐλαχιστότερος: τῷ ἐλαχιστοτέρῳ πάντων. In general the ending τατος tends to disappear. In the New Testament we find this form only once: Acts of the Apostles, xxvi, 5. The superlative is formed by the positive with πολύ. Sometimes the positive is doubled: θεῷ μεγάλῳ μεγάλῳ (Bull. de Corresp. Hellénique, 1894, p. 147—an inscription from the year 91 before Christ), ὁ μέγας καὶ μέγας Ἑρμῆς (CIG. 4697, 19).

The form of the reflexive pronoun of the third person has ousted the forms of the first and second:

---

[1] For example: τοῦ οἰκαίτη = τοῦ οἰκέτου (CIA. 353 3)— Τοῦ Μωησῆ (Exod. xvii, 12).

ἀφ' ἑαυτοῦ σὺ τοῦτο λέγεις (Gospel of St. John, xviii)
instead of ἀπὸ σαυτοῦ.

The indefinite pronoun τις is replaced by εἶς
(cf. in English ' one ' in ' one might say ').

The ending αω of the verbs by degrees ousted
the ending εω and a mixed conjugation is formed:
ἐλεῶ, ἐλεᾶς, ἐλεᾶ, ἐλεοῦμεν, ἐλεᾶτε, ἐλεοῦσι.

The μι-conjugation gives way to the forms of
the ω-conjugation: δίδω = δίδωμι, θέτω = τίθημι.[1]

The optative and the middle are disappearing.
The middle is used, if it must be made plain, that
the action concerns only the agent.

The particle ἄν disappears little by little.

The Syntax

The perfect becomes a purely historical tense
and conflicts with the aorist. In an inscription of
Teos (Cauer [2], 51, 52) we read: Τήιοι ἀπέστειλαν
and some lines farther: Τήιοι ἀπεστάλκαντι (=
ἀπεστάλκασι).

The Ancient Greek rule is well known, that
when the subject is a neuter plural the predicate
must be in the singular. In the κοινή it was so
only if the subject did not signify living objects.
After the subject ἔθνη, for example, the predicate
was put in the plural, because ἔθνη are men and
living objects. The poets of the κοινή-period used
to neglect the Attic rule and the Modern Greek
does not recognize it at all. But on the other side,

[1] Moiris says : ἀπολλύς—'Αττικῶς, ἀπολλύων—'Ελληνικῶς.

we find in the New Testament examples of the
so-called pindaric concordance. If there are many
subjects with a different gender the predicate is
put in the singular: νυνὶ δὲ μένει πίστις, ἐλπίς,
ἀγάπη, τὰ τρία ταῦτα (St. Paul, First Epistle to the
Corinthians, xiii, 13).

It must be observed that in the κοινή some words
have assumed a new signification: λειτουργία does
not signify a financial duty, but divine service;
χρηματίζειν signifies ' to settle officially '; ἀντίληψις
= help; ἐρωτᾶν = to beg; συμβιῶ = to marry;
περίστασις = danger or distress. Some of these
words are preserved in Modern Greek: λοιπόν =
besides. Already in Lucian, Ζεὺς Τραγῳδός, 34:
τί οὖν χρὴ ποιεῖν λοιπόν ;

G

Chapter V

THE VULGAR GREEK

While since the 3rd century before Christ the pure κοινή was the language of all cultivated Greeks, in the mouth of the lower strata of the population a colloquial language was developing and from this Modern Greek is a direct descendant. This is the so-called ' Vulgar Greek '. The term is sometimes used for Modern Greek itself. In any case we must distinguish this language on the one side from the κοινή and on the other from the literary language of Modern Greek, which is generally called καθαρεύουσα, although on both of them there is no doubt it had a very considerable influence. Of its influence on the κοινή we have already spoken. We have also pointed out many peculiarities which have their parallels in Modern Greek; this points to a common source and this source is the Vulgar Greek. In the καθαρεύουσα this influence is still clearer. The infinitive, for example, has completely disappeared, and its place has been taken by the subjunctive introduced by the conjunction νά (= ἵνα). The particle ἄν has also disappeared. Its place has been taken by a new particle: θά (from θέλω νά). The optative does not exist. For the dative εἰς with the accusative is used; sometimes even the simple genitive. Another difference between Vulgar Greek and the κοινή and the καθαρεύουσα is the vocabulary. Vulgar Greek contains a great number of foreign words: French, Italian, Albanian, Slavonic, and Turkish. These are often corrupted to such a degree as to be unrecognizable.[1] In the καθαρεύουσα such of these words as are necessary are given Greek equivalents and these are often artificial to an extreme degree. For example, κραβάτα is not used; its place is taken by λαιμοδεσμός.

As has been said, the development of Vulgar Greek had already begun in antiquity. We know by the aid of inscriptions on vases that in the times when the Attic literature was flourishing, the people did not speak exactly as Demosthenes spoke or as Plato wrote. From the Greek papyri found in Egypt, we now know that the difference between the conversational language used in private correspondence and the literary language in the times of the Ptolemaei was greater still. Barbarisms and blunders violating the rules of Attic grammar are found at every step: ἐπιλανθάνω (instead of ἐπιλανθάνομαι) with accusative (instead of the genitive), ἐπιμέλομαι with dative (instead of the genitive), ἀποστελῶ σε (instead of σοι), etc. Finally Vulgar Greek broke into the literature also, but not before the 6th century of our era are we able to point to any important work written in

---

[1] For example, σαρσένθης = sergeant.

this idiom. This is the chronicle of Malalas, a contemporary of the emperors Zeno, Anastasius I,
Justinus I, and Justinian I. He lived in the 5th
and 6th centuries. Although his work has not
reached us in its primitive form, the editor has
preserved the style and the language of the original.[1]
Isolated examples of the Vulgar Greek we have
also from older times. Very important in this
respect is the literature of the Atticists, i.e. of the
philologers, who from about the beginning of the
Roman Imperial period composed dictionaries for
the use of persons who wished to write correctly
in Attic.[2] Attic words are here translated into the
words of the living language of conversation, of
which in this manner we get a notion. Similarly
very important for the study of the oldest Vulgar
Greek are the Interpretamenta Pseudodositheana,
a Latin-Greek dictionary of the 3rd century of our
era. The Greek words found here belong to the
conventional language of this century. Last of all
we must mention certain phrases and verses
preserved to us as used by the Byzantine mob to
deride and scoff at the vices of some of the emperors.
For example, the party of the Greens in the circus
in the year 608 saluted the emperor Phokas with
the following words: πάλιν 's τὸν καῦκον ἔπιες,

---

[1] Cf. K. Wolf, *Studien zur Sprache des Malalas*, 1914.
[2] We possess the ὀνομαστικόν of Pollux, the λέξεις τῶν δέκα
ῥητόρων of Harpokration, the λέξεις Ἀττικαί of Moiris,
the ἐκλογή of the Ἀττικιστής of Phrynichos, and the so-called
Ἀντιαττικιστής perhaps of the same author.

πάλιν τὸν νοῦν ἀπώλεσας. The word καῦκος belongs exclusively to the Vulgar Greek and signifies ' a cup ' or also a ' lover ' (cf. Gustav Meyer in the *Byzantinische Zeitschrift*, vol. iii (1894), p. 162). The verse may be translated: ' Again thou art drunken; again thou hast lost thy senses.' In this fragment also the abbreviation 'ς must be noticed (instead of εἰς); it is common in Modern Greek. Further, in the satirical verses on the emperor Maurice sung about the year 600, we may remark the expression τὸ καινὸν ἀλεκτόριν and the word ξυλοκούκουδα. The form ἀλεκτόριν is an abbreviation of ἀλεκτόριον, a diminutive of ἀλέκτωρ. This form in ιν, which we find in the Byzantine ballads (ἄσματα δημοτικά), for example in the τοῦ 'Αρμούρη ἄσμα (v. 4—τὸ παιδίν = τὸ παιδίον and v. 15— 'Αρμουροπουλίν), is a transitional form from the ιον of Ancient to the ι of Modern Greek. The compounded word ξυλοκούκουδα contains firstly the word ξύλον. The word κούκουδα is evidently kindred to the modern expressions κουκκοῦλα (cf. the Latin *cucculus* = a hood, in German *Gugel*), κουκκου- λόνω, κουκκούλωμα.[1] The sons of the emperor were called ' masked logs of wood '; this means that they were as stupid as logs.[2]

Very important for the study of the older Vulgar Greek would be the popular songs and epic poems

---

[1] The transition of λ to δ is known already in the antiquity. Besides cf. *poddi* = πολύ in the modern Greek dialects in southern Italy.

[2] One might compare the English word *blockhead*.

of the Byzantine period. But the former are completely lost to us, and the epic poems are not preserved in their primitive form. The oldest manu-
script of the poem of Digenis Akritas is not older
than the 14th century. Our literary material for
Vulgar Greek from the 6th century until the 10th
is very scanty: some legends of saints (for example,
the Life of Symeon by Leontios Neapolitanus of
the 7th century), the romance of Barlaam and
Josaphat, and the chronicle of Theophanes. From
the 10th century we have the writings of the
emperor Constantinus Porphyrogennetos and the
official Byzantine deeds from Italy composed in
the language of this period. From the 11th century
all writings intended to circulate among the larger
part of the public were written in Vulgar Greek.
Thus the so-called Σπανέας, a book containing
practical rules for the household, is written precisely
in this language. The literary language was then
already totally forgotten and unintelligible to the
majority of the nation.

In the historical literature of the Byzantine
authors we find two different languages. Books
destined for a small intelligent circle of readers
were composed in the κοινή or even in Attic. On
the other hand, the popular chronicles, which were
intended to satisfy the curiosity of the wider
public, were written in a more or less modified type
of Vulgar Greek.[1] But the purest Vulgar Greek we

[1] D. Psaltes, *Die Sprache der byzantinischen Chronisten.*

find in the verse-chronicles, for example, in the Chronicle of Morea, which was composed in the 13th century, in the documents of the archives and in the ballads (ἄσματα δημοτικά), of which a considerable number has been preserved dating from the 10th to the 16th century.[1]

[1] Collections by Passow (*Popularia carmina græca*) and Legrand (*Recueil de chansons populaires grecques*).

Chapter VI

MODERN GREEK

From what we have already said, it is plain that in the Vulgar Greek certain forms of speech began to appear, which have now in Modern Greek become regular and normal. Modern Greek being in fact a development from this Vulgar Greek. But in addition a certain influence of the ancient dialects must be recognized : the ending ες, for example, of the accusative plural of the third declension is a feature of the ancient dialects of Elis, of Delphi, and of Phthiotis. To lay down any precise chronological limit between Vulgar and Modern Greek is even more difficult than to say when Ancient Greek ended and the κοινή began. It is usually said that the Modern Greek language and literature began in the 15th century, although some scholars prefer a considerably earlier date.[1]

---

[1] Hatzidakis supposes that the modern period began as early as the 11th century. In regard to the vocabulary the date of the development of Modern Greek can be pushed back even to antiquity. In the Salt-papyrus in the Museum of the Louvre has come down to us a note-book of a Roman of the 2nd century of our era with the translation of Latin words into the colloquial speech of the time, and here we find already quite modern Greek words : *pane(m)* = *oxomin* (= *to psomin* = τὸ ψωμί), *ventre(m)* = *cilia* (κοιλιά), *piscem* = *opsari* (τὸ ψάρι), *oleum* = *eladi* (= τὸ λάδι). Also in the New Testament we find Modern Greek words : ὀψάριον = fish (τὸ ψάρι), βρέχει = it rains, μεσητεύω = I am mediating.

Modern Greek owes its characteristic features partly to its special grammar, in which there are many new forms and constructions altogether unknown to the ancient language, and partly to its vocabulary, into which many foreign elements have found their way. But in general it may be laid down that Modern Greek bears a much closer resemblance to the ancient form of the language than the Romance languages have to Latin. Except some of the dialects, the form of the words is much less changed.

Phonetics

The historical study of the phonetics of a language is rendered difficult by the circumstance that we can, properly speaking, study directly only the sounds of the living language, while the sounds of the language of the past are expressed for us only under the form of dead letters. Thus historical phonetics is reduced to the study of the signification of the letters in the different periods of the development of a language, for the letters have not always signified the same sounds. Sometimes the manner of writing a word is changed together with its pronunciation. But usually the latter moves more quickly than the former; the writing changes slower. This is evident, if we remember that each single letter was at first intended to correspond to a certain sound. Now we perceive that in modern languages often two or

three letters express only one sound. This is the
case in English, in French, and also in Modern
Greek. This proves that originally the words were
pronounced otherwise than they are to-day. We
possess evidence that this was actually so. Erasmus
of Rotterdam living in the 16th century is a
witness that in the French word *beau* each of the
three vowels was audible. To-day the French
pronounce it with but one vowel: *o* (*bo*). In the
same way in the time of Erasmus in the words
feu and *peu*, both vowels, *e* and *u*, were audible,
whilst to-day we hear but one sound corresponding
to the English *u* in 'tub' or 'cup.' In the same
century the English word 'mane' was pronounced
with a pure *a* as in 'far' or 'father.' Shakespeare
rhymes the words 'foppish' and 'apish'; the
latter word, therefore, was pronounced with an *a*
sounding like in 'all' or 'fall,' not as it is pronounced to-day.

In Modern Greek the sound *i*, for example, is
written ι, η, οι, ει, and υ, but originally these
letters indicated each of them a different sound.
Our task is now to show how the letters used in
modern Greek originally were pronounced and
how they are pronounced to-day.

The letter ᾱ, marking a long *a*, was in antiquity
pronounced purely only by the Dorians and
partly by the Æolians. The latter pronounced it
as a sound tending towards *o*, if it happened to be
near either of the consonants ν or ρ. In this case

they also wrote the sound with an o ($\sigma\tau\rho\sigma\tau\acute{o}s$ = $\sigma\tau\alpha\tau\acute{o}s$). The Ionians pronounced it as a sound tending towards E, as in the English also a is pronounced in ' lake ' or ' fate ', and used for it the letter H, which originally marked an aspiration, as in Latin, and was called ' Heth '. Since the spiritus at the beginning of words was lost in Ionian, the letter was called '*eth* or $^*H\tau\alpha$ and was used for the aforesaid sound.[1] That H was in fact a representative of A appears from this, that where we have in Dorian α, in Ionian we have η: $\delta\hat{\alpha}\mu os$—$\delta\hat{\eta}\mu os$, $o\grave{\iota}\kappa\acute{\iota}\alpha$—$o\grave{\iota}\kappa\acute{\iota}\eta$. After the 4th century before Christ in the inscriptions η was often confounded with ϵ or with $\epsilon\iota$. We read in Attic inscriptions $\kappa\lambda\epsilon\acute{\iota}s$ instead of the primitive $\kappa\lambda\acute{\eta}\iota s$ (the original form was *$\kappa\lambda\acute{\alpha}F\iota s$; cf. the Latin *clavis*), $\grave{\epsilon}\nu\epsilon\hat{\iota}\sigma\alpha\nu$ instead of $\grave{\epsilon}\nu\hat{\eta}\sigma\alpha\nu$.[2] We infer that the pronunciation of the H then approached the French *é fermé*, i.e. a sound between E and I (in ' pin '). In the 2nd century before Christ η was pronounced already directly as I in Bœotia. Instead of $\grave{\alpha}\delta\iota\kappa\hat{\eta}$ in inscriptions we find $\grave{\alpha}\delta\iota\kappa\hat{\iota}$. In Attica the process of this metamorphose was slower. The confusion of η and ι did not begin in Attica until the 2nd century of our era: $X\alpha\rho\acute{\eta}\sigma\iota os$ instead of $X\alpha\rho\acute{\iota}\sigma\iota os$. But cultivated people continued

[1] Cf. the Latin *erus* for *herus* and the English ' 'at ' for ' hat.'
[2] That the long $\bar{e}$ was written as $\epsilon\iota$ may be explained by the fact that after a drawled $\bar{e}$ we hear an i. The same may be said of $\bar{o}$ and its expression by oi. Thence we read $\grave{\eta}\gamma\nu o\acute{\iota}\eta\sigma\epsilon\nu$ in Homer instead of $\grave{\eta}\gamma\nu\acute{o}\eta\sigma\epsilon\nu$. Cf. also papyrus of Herodas, v. 72, $\acute{\upsilon}\pi o\nu o\iota\epsilon\hat{\iota}s$ instead of $\acute{\upsilon}\pi o\nu o\epsilon\hat{\iota}s$.

to pronounce H as E even in the 4th century of
our era. The translator of the Bible, the Goth
Ulfilas, transcribes in this century the Greek η with e.
This we observe also in the Armenian translation
of the Holy Scripture. Even to-day in the Pontic
dialect of Modern Greek η sounds as E and is
written with an ϵ: $\dot{\epsilon}\phi\dot{\epsilon}\kappa\alpha = \dot{\alpha}\phi\hat{\eta}\kappa\alpha$, $\pi\epsilon\gamma\acute{\alpha}\delta\iota = \pi\eta\gamma\acute{\eta}$.

In the same way, just as η was originally used
to express a sound intermediate between A and E,
so the letter ω (a doubled O) expressed a sound
between A and O like the English a in ' water.'
The letter O signified a pure O. Later this difference
in the pronunciation of ω and o gradually disappeared. Already from the 3rd century before
Christ in the Egyptian papyri these letters are
sometimes confused: $\dot{\omega}\kappa\tau\alpha\epsilon\tau\eta\rho\acute{\iota}s$, $\ddot{\epsilon}\delta o\kappa\alpha$, $\dot{\omega}\rho\hat{\alpha}\tau\alpha\iota$,
$\dot{o}\mu\nu\acute{v}o$. In an inscription of Magnesia of the 2nd
century before Christ, we read $'A\rho\tau\epsilon\mu\iota\delta\acute{o}\rho o\nu$ instead
of $'A\rho\tau\epsilon\mu\iota\delta\acute{\omega}\rho o\nu$, and in an inscription of the 1st
century—$\phi\iota\lambda o\delta\acute{\omega}\xi\omega s$.[1] But cultivated people were
certainly still able to distinguish these letters and
sounds in the 1st century of our era: evidence of
this is the play upon the words mōrari and mŭrari
in a remark of the emperor Nero concerning
Claudius (cf. Sueton, *Nero*, 33). Nowadays there
is no difference of pronunciation of ω and o and
of η and ι.

The letter v originally signified the sound U,

[1] Cf. E. Nachmanson, *Laute der magnesischen Inschriften*,
p. 64.

as in the English ' flute.' This pronunciation
is preserved in some words even in Modern
Greek: μουστάκι = μύσταξ, γρουστάλλι = κρύσταλλος,[1]
οὐγρός = ὑγρός. In antiquity the υ was still
pronounced thus in the 4th century before Christ
in Bœotia and Laconia, while in other Greek regions
this letter represented a sound between U and I.
The pure U was expressed by ου. Having adopted
this orthography the Bœotians and Laconians
wrote from about 400 before Christ—κάρουα
instead of κάρυα, διούο instead of later δύο, that is υ
was pronounced as U and as I U. It is known that
V in the Italic dialects has precisely this use.[2]
Further, the sound developed like y in the direction
of I. A sound between U and I was Y. The existence
of this sound is to be discerned very early in Attica.
In early writings we find before Y the letter K
and not Ϙ (the koppa); from this we may infer
that Y was pronounced y and not u: on the one
hand we have, for example, Κύλον, and on the
other—ϘΟΡΕΙ (= κόρη). Then we meet the
confusion of υ and ι in many words, as in 'Αμφικ-
τίονες, which was also written 'Αμφικτύονες,
and in ἥμισυ, also written ἥμνυν. The word κίνδυνος
was originally written κύνδυνος. This fluctuation
between Y and I is very old and lasted a very
long time.[3] Plutarch in the 2nd century of our

---

[1] In Russian *Chrustalj*.

[2] In an Oscan inscription at Messina we read : *Njumsdieis* =
Numerii.

[3] Cf. Karl Meister, *Die homerische Kunstsprache*, pp. 147–182,
and in *Kuhns Zeitschrift*, i–ii, 207.

era transcribed the Roman name ' Bibulus ' by
Βύβλος, and in the 10th century Suidas in his
dictionary brought together as under one initial
all the words beginning with ι, η, and ει, which
letters in his day had the same sound I, but he
entered under a separate heading all the words
beginning with υ. Even at the present day in some
dialects (in Trebizona and also in Attica) υ is
pronounced as Y. The Zakonians pronounce it
as ju: τjούχα = τύχη, ἄχjουρο = ἄχυρον, and in
southern Italy the Greeks—as a pure U: κšούλα =
ξύλα.

Since υ was tending towards the sound of Y or I,
the Greeks used for a pure U the letters ου, which
originally expressed an O tending to U; instead
of *μισθόομεν they wrote μισθοῦμεν and instead of
μο(ι) ἐστίν—μοῦστίν.[1]

As I have already said, the sound I in Modern
Greek is rendered also by ει. Originally the two
vowels were here audible separately, but very
early the transition to one sound was brought
down, the sound ε being very nearly related to I.
In Modern Greek very often we find ι instead of ε :
ἤθελι = ἤθελε, ἔπιρνι = ἔπαιρνε (αι = ε). As early
as the 5th century before Christ in inscriptions ει
was confused with ι : ἀφαιρῖσθαι = ἀφαιρεῖσθαι,
Χαρικλίδας = Χαρικλείδας, Χίρων = Χείρων. Examples
are found also in the text of Aristophanes : στυπειο-

---

[1] This is the origin of μου as dative (instead of μοι) in Modern
Greek (cf. below).

πώλης = στυππιοπώλης (*Equites*, 129), ὀπτάνιον = ὀπτάνειον (*Pax*, 891). If we suppose that ει and ι sounded alike, we may recognize a comic repetition of sound in Εὐριπίδη'πειδήπερ (*Acharnes*, 437). While in general ει was tending towards ι, on the other side before ρ, α, and ο we have to remark a tendency towards ε: χέρα = χεῖρα, πορέα = πορεία, διδασκαλέα = διδασκαλεῖα, 'Αλεξανδρέα = 'Αλεξανδρεία. As is well known, the Romans wrote: Æneas = Αἰνείας, Medea = Μήδεια, but on the other side, Darius (Δαρεῖος), Alexandria = 'Αλεξανδρεία. In Modern Greek ει is exclusively pronounced as ι.

Further, the diphthong οι is at present pronounced in the same manner. In the 5th century before Christ in Bœotia it was written οε-Μοεριχος = Μοίριχος, and similarly in Attica—Κροεσος = Κροῖσος. As is known, the Romans always wrote Crœsus. In Greece the two vowels in οε were separately audible, like in the Celtic oë. On the other hand, we observe before vowels a development of οι towards O [1] and later towards U and Y. Indeed, we meet in Bœotia usually the orthography υ = οι. From the 2nd century before Christ this orthography is found also elsewhere: the ending ηιοις was written νυς (cf. πυήσουσι = ποιήσουσι). From Y the sound of υ became i, and this is the usual pronunciation of it in Modern Greek.

---

[1] For example, in the papyrus of Menander (Heros, v. 72) we read ὑπονοιεῖς instead of ὑπονοεῖς. In general in all Indo-European languages the diphthongs have a tendency to become simple vowels. Cf. the Latin and the Roman languages.

The diphthong αι had a propensity to become
αεj; cf. the transition of α to η, i.e. to a sound
between A and E. In inscriptions on Corinthian
vases of the 5th century before Christ we read
Αθαναεια = 'Αθαναία. Later the ι was no longer
heard: in Bœotia we read ἐπὶ 'Αμεινοκλειαε
(instead of ἐπὶ 'Αμεινοκλείαι). Also in Attica on a
vase we read Αεθρα = Αἴθρα. The Romans wrote
the Greek αι always as ae : Thraex = Θρᾶιξ. In
Bœotia from the 4th century before Christ, η was
written instead of αι, i.e. a sound between A and E
(cf. above). In Modern Greek αι sounds exactly
as ε, which sound passes often (before vowels)
to j: παλjός = παλαιός.[1]

In the diphthongs αυ and ευ the vowels originally
sounded separately. Even in the 3rd century before
Christ instead of αυ—αο was sometimes written and
instead of ευ—εο : ἀοτός (= αὐτός), εόνοια (= εὔνοια).
On the other hand, instead of Σωκράτης (originally
*Σαοκράτης from σάος = salvus), in Bœotia we
find Σαυκράτης. But later the thin vowels α and ε
preponderated and the sound υ = U became a
spirant (Ŭ). Then it approached the sound called
digamma (= the English w or wh) and was then
written like this (F) or on the other hand, where the
digamma should be written the υ was placed:
εὔαδε = ἔϜαδε (from Ϝανδάνω = ἀνδάνω), ἔκαυσα =

---

[1] From the transition of A to E and I we can explain the
formation of τις instead of τας in Modern Greek : τας, ταις
(τες), τις.

ἔκαϝσα (from *καϝjο = καίω). Finally only the thin vowels remained. Already in the 1st century of our era ἀτοῦ was written instead of αὐτοῦ and ἑατοῦ instead of ἑαυτοῦ. In Modern Greek out of ἀτοῦ—τοῦ was developed.[1] In other cases the υ has become a consonant = the Latin v, a stage of this progress having apparently been the digamma.[2] Before β, γ, δ, λ, μ, ν, ρ, and ζ—υ is at present sounded as V, and before π, κ, τ, φ, χ, θ, and ς by way of assimilation—as F. In colloquial language, ev and ef early became changed to ep. In a papyrus of the year 159 before Christ it is written ἐμβλεύσαντες instead of ἐμβλέψαντες. In Modern Greek ἐπαίδευσα is pronounced as ἐπαίδεψα.—Beside the vowels in Greek there existed also semi-vowels, namely ĭ, ž, and ŭ. The former two disappeared at an early date, which is evident from the fact that there are no peculiar letters for them. Their existence can be proved only by comparing Greek words with words of other languages and by some phonetic traces which appear in the writing.

The semi-vowel ĭ must be distinguished from the consonant j. The former in the beginning of words has become a spiritus asper: ὑσμίνη, originally ἰυσμίνη—from the stem yudh (= ' to fight ' in Sanscrit). In the middle of words ĭ disappeared or a diphthong was formed with the preceding

---

[1] For example : ὁ πατέρας τοῦ = ὁ πατὴρ αὐτοῦ. In Asia Minor the ending of ἀτοῦ is omitted : τὸν υἱόνατ = τὸν υἱὸν αὐτοῦ.
[2] Cicero pronounced the name Καυνέας—cav'neeas (de divinatione, ii, 84).

vowel: θυίω, θείην. After a consonant ἰ became even a pure vowel, ἰδίω, from sϜιδίω, in Sanscrit *svidyami*, in English ' to sweat,' in German *schwitzen*.—The consonant *j*, the existence of which in later times is shown by the metrical shortening of οι and αι before vowels, ποјεῖ, τοјοῦτος, in the beginning of words changed to ζ: ζυγόν (cf. in Latin *iugum*, in English ' yoke,' in German *Joch*), ζωμός (cf. in Sanscrit *yūsa*, in Slavonic *yuchá*, in Russian *uchá*).[1] Internally λj became λλ (φύλλον, cf. the Latin *folium*), *d + j — ζ* (pronounced *ds*; cf. Djauš in Sanscrit = Ζεύς), *g + j — ζ*, *t + j — τσ — σ* (*πάντjα = πᾶσα), *νj — νν* (*κτένjω—*κτέννω —κτείνω), *πj — t, dj — σσ*.

The original existence in Greek of the semi-vowel ž can be proved by comparing the Greek word μισθός with the word *mizhdem* in Avesta, *mizdo* in Gothic, and *mzdá* in Slavonic. We see that the semi-vowel ž has become in Greek the consonant σ. But before μ, ν, ρ,—β, γ, δ to-day σ sounds as *z*: πιστεύω 's μίαν—ἐκκλησίαν sounds π. *zmian*—ἐκκλησίαν. The word σβύνω sounds *zwino*. In antiquity in Attic inscriptions we find a confusion of σ and ζ: Ζμύρνα = Σμύρνα, ἀναβαζμούς = ἀναβασμούς. Cf. also Waddington, *Inscriptions de la Syric*, 2413*b*.

While of the semi-vowels ἰ and ž but few traces have remained in Greek, the semi-vowel ŭ expressed

---

[1] But sometimes *j* appears in Greek as spiritus asper: cf. in Sanscrit *yas*, and Appendix I, 2.

by the letter Ϝ (the digamma) was until the 5th century before Christ a living sound in almost all the Greek dialects; in Æolian and partly in Dorian it lasted even longer.[1] The special letter, with which it was marked, was called a double gamma in consequence of its shape, and occupied the sixth place in the Greek alphabet. Later the sound was marked in some dialects (before ρ) by a β; it became a consonant. Originally the pronunciation of the digamma was similar to the English *w* or *wh* (for example, in ' world ' or ' wheel '); this is evident from the etymology of the words in which it occurred. Besides it was confounded with *v* (= *ŭ*). After its disappearance the digamma sometimes left a trace (τέτταρες from *τέτϜαρες; cf. in Sanscrit *ca-tváras*, in Russian *cetvertyi*; ὑποδδείσας from *ὑποδϜείσας; εἶδαρ from *ἔδϜαρ). The poets neglected the elision before words beginning formerly with a digamma. Sometimes at the beginning of a word the digamma was replaced by the spiritus asper: (1) if in the next syllable there was a *s* instead of the primitive *h* (ἱμάτιον, cf. primitively *Ϝισμάτιον, in Latin *vestis* from the Indo-European *wsma or *whma); (2) if σ or ρ + *a* mute consonant followed: ἕσπερος from *Ϝέσπερος; cf. in Latin *vesper*; ἑστία, cf. Vesta; ἔρση, cf. in Sanscrit *varšám*.

The consonant β = ϐ was early pronounced as a

---

[1] In Ionian the digamma disappeared very early. In Homer it has disappeared before ο, ω, and ου.

spiranted sound. Already in the 3rd century before Christ β appears sometimes instead of the digamma (ǔ): βαστίας (from Ϝάστυ), Εὐρυβάνασσα (from Ϝάνασσα = ἄνασσα, the feminine of ἄναξ), βοικία (= Ϝοικία; cf. the Latin *vicus*). It was very natural for the pronunciation to pass to the English *w* and then to the consonant *v*, as β is in fact pronounced in Modern Greek. Where the pure *B* is wanted the Greeks write now μπ: μπαλκόνι, μπαστοῦνι (cf. the French *le baton*; in Old French *le baston*).

The liquid ρ was in antiquity aspirated: ΡΗΟϜΑΙΣΙ (*Inscr. of Corcyra*, vi, s.B.Chr.).

Similarly, γ was early pronounced as a spiranted sound and approached the sound *ju*. In Bœotia instead of ἐγώ(ν) we find ἰών = in Sanscrit *aham*. Rhinthon (3rd century before Christ) writes: ὀλίος = ὀλίjγος = ὀλίγος. In Modern Greek γ is *j* before *I* and ε: γυναῖκα, γέρος = *junaîka, jéros*. Before other vowels γ is pronounced as a spiranted *g*—*gh*: γάτα—*ghátā* (the cat).

It must be mentioned that γ sometimes occupies the place of ν in Greek words, namely before γ, κ, χ, ξ. Before ξ and χ it marks a nasal sound like the *n* in the French words *mon* or *ton*: συγχωρῶ. The letters κγ and γγ are pronounced *ng*: ἄγγελος—*angelos*. This represents the gutturonasal ñ, which existed by the side of the labionasal (*m*) and the dental nasal (*n*). The gutturonasal is, for example, still clearly perceivable in the following expression

of the Lord's prayer: τῶν ἀλλωνῶν τὶς ἁμαρτίες =
ton alonō̃ dis amarties.[1]

The so-called irrational γ marks an aspiration:
ἀγώρι = ἄωρος = a young boy (from ὥρα and the
α privativum).

Similarly δ early became a spiranted sound = *th*
in the English word ' this.' Already in antiquity
in an inscription of Olympia we read ζίκαια =
δίκαια.[2]

Only after a nasal the δ has always preserved
its primitive pronunciation as a pure *d*. Generally
δ is pronounced in Modern Greek as a spirant:
γίδα = *jidha*, but as *dz* before ι and ν (= *i*).

In the spoken Modern Greek the ν in the ending
of words is ousted[3]; the following mediæ, δ, β,
and γ, are changed in spirants: *to vasiljá* (= τὸν
βασιλέα), *to dulo* (τὸν δοῦλον), *to Zámbro* (τὸν γαμπρόν).
Already in the κοινή the ν in the ending was
pronounced feebly τὸ(ν) υόν.

The spirants χ, φ, and θ were pronounced in
antiquity as tenues aspiratæ. The Romans transcribed χ by *Ch* (*c* sounded in Rome as *k*), φ by *Ph*,
and θ by *Th*: Chrysippus (= Χρύσιππος),[4] Philippus
(= Φίλιππος), Theodorus (= Θεόδωρος). As appears

---

[1] The tenues become mediæ after nasals.

[2] In Laconia, on the contrary, instead of ζωμός we find δωμός
(*Etym. Magnum*, p. 316, 56). Apparently the pronunciation was
fluctuating.

[3] It is preserved in the article τὸν τήν, in αὐτόν, in δέν, ἄν,
σάν, πρίν before vowels and κ, π, τ, ξ, ψ, τσ.

[4] This Latin orthography sometimes was accepted also in
the Greek East: ἐκχθρότατα (Dittenberger, *Sylloge*, i, 328).

from a story told by Quintilian, the Greeks pronounced the Roman name Fundanius—Phundanius. The same pronunciation appears also from the elision ἐφ' ᾧ instead of ἐπ' ᾧ (ἐπὶ ᾧ), and the same is proved by the form γέγραπται instead of *γέγραφται (from γράπhω = γράφω). In Modern Greek φ sounds as a spirant. From the evidence of Priscian we know that this same pronunciation was in use about the year A.D. 500. In Modern Greek χ sounds still as a guttural: *Kh*. The modern name of the island Χίος is Σκιό from 's τὴ Χίο(ν) = 's (τὴ) *Khío*.

The compound letters ξ and ψ were originally pronounced *chs* and *phs*. In Ancient Greek local alphabets which did not possess these letters, χσ and φσ were used instead: ἔδοχσεν = ἔδοξεν, φσέφισμα = ψήφισμα. In Modern Greek traces of the spiranted pronunciation are sometimes perceivable: ὀχ instead of ἐκ. Generally ξ and ψ are nowadays pronounced as *ks* and *ps*.

In antiquity the sounds expressed by θ and ζ were also of a double nature. The original pronunciation of θ was *t-h* (an aspirated *t*). On a vase we read Θαλhύβιος instead of Θαλθύβιος (= Ταλθύβιος). In Modern Greek θ is a dental sibilant = the English *th* in ' think.' Also ζ was in antiquity a double sound: *ds* or *sd*. The latter pronunciation appears from a passage in Sextus Empiricus, who says that no Greek word can end with a ζ because no Greek word ends with a double consonant. The same pronunciation is attested also by some etymologies: ὄζος, cf. the Gothic *asts*, the German *Ast*, the Armenian *ost*—sounded *osdos*.[1] ἀζάλεος, cf. tshekhian *ozd* (malt kiln). Further, the preposition σύν loses in Attic its ν before ζ, which can only be explained if ζ was *sd*, not *ds*. Cf. συ(ν) σπάω and συ(ν) ζεύγνυμι. Lastly, instead of Θεόσδοτος we read also Θεόζοτος, ἔζων = ἔστων (Wescher-Foucart, *Inscriptions de Delphes*, nr. 189, 13). The Persian names Auramasda and Artavasdes were transcribed in Greek Ὠρομάζης and Ἀρταουάζης. But we know from the ancient grammarians that the pronunciation of zeta as *ds* gradually prevailed, after the sound was simplified and pronounced simply as the voiced *s*, as in the German word *so*. This is the pronunciation of zeta in Modern Greek. But it was already found in ancient times. In a papyrus we read ἐζύγη instead of ἐσύγη, in another νομίζαντα instead of νομίσαντα, and in an Attic inscription—ψηφίσεσθαι instead of ψηφίζεσθαι; further: ἐχυράσουσιν = ἐχυράζουσιν, Σεύς = Ζεύς (in Modern Greek Zεfs). We must mention also the writing Πελαζγικόν = Πελασγικόν and ζεμέλω = the earth (in Phrygian; cf. in Russian *zemljá*).

In addition to the unvoiced and voiced sibilants (the sigma and zeta) we find in some of the Modern Greek dialects a sound resembling the English *sh* (*ś*). Whether this sound existed anywhere in Ancient

---

[1] Lagercrantz (*Griech. Lautgeschichte*, p. 132) proposes another etymology: ὄζος = *Fόδιος = the Anglo-Saxon *watol* and the English ' wattle.'

Greek or whether it has been borrowed later from neighbouring languages (Slavonic, Turkish, or Armenian) we have no means of knowing. The latter supposition is the more probable, because if such a sound had existed in antiquity, a peculiar letter would have been invented to express it. Some scholars (like Lagercrantz in *Zur griech. Laut-geschichte*) maintain that the letter M (i.e. Σ on the side) found in Greek inscriptions should be pronounced as *sh*. But this letter is never found in the same inscription as the Σ, and this would be the only really cogent reason which would compel us to suppose that they too had different sounds.[1]

The pronunciation of the tenues π, κ, τ has changed since antiquity in the sense that the difference between the velar and palatal κ (between κ and ϙ) very early grew indistinct, and that before *t* the tenues π and κ have now become spirants: ἑφτά = ἑπτά, ὀχτώ = ὀκτώ. After a nasal κ and τ are pronounced as a *gh* and *d*: Πάγκαλος = Pan-ghalos, τὸν κύριον = *ton ghirion*, πέντε = *pende*. Similarly after μ, π is pronounced as a β: ἔμπορος = *emboros*.

Morphology

As in most languages, the inflexion of the substantives and adjectives is in Greek on the way to be completely lost. But in Greek this

---

[1] Professor R. M. Dawkins of Oxford suggests that the sound *sh* may have developed inside Greek in the mediæval period (personal communication).

process has not gone so far as in the Romance languages and English, where the noun is unchanged and the function of the cases is taken over by the prepositions. In Greek, as in German, we have before us only a tendency towards this kind of declension or, to speak more accurately, towards this substitute for declension. The endings of the cases have not yet become obsolete with the exception of the dative.[1] This case is replaced by the accusative with the preposition εἰς, 's ('s) or the genitive or even the simple accusative.[2] The genitive is sometimes replaced by the accusative with the preposition ἀπό. In the plural it is always so, except of some dialects, where the ending of the genitive ωνε (ων) occurs, or (in Samos) οῦνις.

The substantives of the *masculine* gender have the following endings : ος, ης, ῆς, ας, ᾶς, ις, ες, and οῦς. The declension of substantives in ος corresponds to the old second declension (stems on O), only the ν in the ending is omitted : φίλο(ν), φίλω(ν). Besides the vocative in ε, there is also a vocative in ο

---

[1] K. Dieterich (in *Untersuchungen zur Geschichte der griech. Sprache in der hellenistischen Zeit bis zum 10 Jahrhundert*, Leipzig, 1898) states the following reasons for the disappearance of the forms of the dative in Greek : (1) The monophthongization of diphthongs, which appears early, especially in Egypt ; (2) the fact that the long and short vowels grow equal in pronunciation ($ω = o$) ; (3) the disappearance of the ν in the ending ($τὸ(μ)\ λόγο(ν) = τῷ\ λόγῳ$). All these phenomena are observed especially since the 2nd century A.D.

[2] Already in antiquity occur instances like the following : γράφωμαι σε (= σοι), Grenfell and Hunt, ii, 38 (81 b. Chr.), τὴν μεσημβρίαν = τῇ μεσημβρίᾳ (Genesis, xliii, 15, *dativus temporis*), χθὲς ὥραν ἑβδόμην = ὥρᾳ ἑβδόμῃ (Joann. iv, 52).

through the Italian influence: λοῦστρο (the boot black); cf. the Latin verb *lustrare*.

The words in ης have in the genitive, accusative, and vocative singular the ending η, and in the nominative, accusative, and vocative plural— ες or αις (for ες and αις are pronounced in the same manner): ὁ κλέφτης (= κλέπτης), τοῦ κλέφτη, 's τὸν κλέφτη, τὸν κλέφτη(ν), ὦ κλέφτη; οἱ κλέφταις, τῶν κλεφτῶν, 's τοὺς κλέφταις, τοὺς κλέφταις, ὦ κλέφταις. In the same manner are declined the substantives in ας, but with the stem α: ὁ πατέρας, τοῦ πατέρα, etc.

The words in ῆς are declined in the following manner: παπουτζῆς (shoemaker), παπουτζῆ, etc.; παπουτζῆδες,[1] παπουτζήδω, παπουτζῆδες, etc.

The words in ᾶς, ις, ες, and οῦς are declined in the same manner with the stems α, ι, ε, and ου.

The substantives of the *feminine* gender have the endings α, η, οῦ, ε, ο, and ω.

The words in α have in the genitive ᾶς or ας, in the accusative—α, in the nominative and accusative plural—ες,[2] in the genitive plural ῶ(νε) or, if the word was in Ancient Greek declined in the third declension—ω(ν). Some words of the ancient third declension in the form of the accusative on α, τὴν γυναῖκα, have become nominatives on α: ἡ γυναῖκα. The words in η and ι are declined similarly. The words in ι have in the genitive the ending ις: ἡ βρύσι (source), τῆς βρύσις.

---

[1] By analogy with the dental stems.   [2] Since the 10th century.

The words in οῦ (ἀλεποῦ = ἀλώπηξ) have in the genitive the ending οῦς, in the accusative—οῦ, in the nominative and accusative of the plural οῦδες,[1] and in the genitive of the plural—οῦδω(ν). The words in έ are declined similarly (νενέ = grand-mother,[2] νενές; νενέδες, νενέδω).

Neuter words have the endings ο, ιο (ειο, jο), ι, ιμο, ος, μα, and ας.

The words in ο, ιο, and ι are declined as in the old second declension. The words in ιμο and ας have the stem in ατ, as the neuters in μα (ὀνόματ-ος): τὸ γράψιμο(ν), τοῦ γραψιμάτου; τὸ κρέας, τοῦ κρέατος. The neuters in ος are declined as those of the ancient third declension (τὸ τεῖχος); only in the plural instead of the ending η the ending ια (τὰ σκέλη—τὰ σκέληα—σκέλεα) also occurs, and the genitive singular has the ending ος instead of ους.[3]

The adjectives have the following endings: ος (fem. η, and if the ending of the masculine is jος—α, neuter—ο), ύς (fem. ειά, neuter ύ: γλυκύς, γλυκειά, γλυκύ), ις (fem. α, neuter ικο: γρινjάρις, γρινjάρα, γρινjάρικο).

The declension of the adjectives is the same as that of the substantives with the same endings; but the feminine in α of the ις-adjectives forms the plural in ες (instead of ιδες).

The *comparative* endings of adjectives in ος and

---

[1] By analogy with the dental stems.
[2] Cf. in Russian: *njánja* = the nurse.
[3] *Papyrus of the Louvre*, 317 (A.D. 154): τοῦ μέρος.

ύς are οτερος (or ωτερος as in Ancient Greek) and ύτερος. The ancient superlative ending τατος does not exist. The *superlative* is formed from the comparative by prefixing the article: ὁ μικρότερος (= ὁ μικρότατος in ancient Greek).[1]

The adjectives in ις and ης form the comparative by prefixing πjó (= πλεῖον): πjò γρινjάρις. In the superlative the article is prefixed: ὁ πjò γρινjάρις.

Adverbs from adjectives are formed by substituting the ending α: καλός, καλά—and this α is in general ending of all adverbs; for example, μακρειά = far. Already in antiquity such adverbs can be found: ἀνειμένα πολιορκούμενοι (*Agathias*, 52, 25), ἀλέκτορα ἕτοιμα θές (*Papyrus Leidensis*, ii w, p. 10a, line 48).

The *personal pronouns* are ἐγώ, ἐσύ, αὐτός. In declension we must distinguish between the conjunctive and disjunctive forms of these pronouns, as in French between les pronoms conjoints et disjoints. The disjunctive forms are used only for purposes of emphasis: ἐσὺ εἶσαι; = is it thou? (= no other?).

The first and second persons are declined as follows: (i) ἐγώ, ἐμένα, ἐμένα-ἐμεῖς, ἐμᾶς, ἐμᾶς; (ii) ἐσύ, ἐσένα, ἐσένα-ἐσεῖς, ἐσᾶς, ἐσᾶς. The forms ἐμένα and ἐσένα are developed from the old accusatives ἐμέ and σε by adding α, the ending of the accusative singular of the substantives of the

---

[1] This manner of forming the superlative occurs sometimes in ancient Greek: τὴν ἀμείνω τῶν μοιρῶν (Lucian, *Dialogi deorum*, 204).

third declension. To the form *σένα was also
prefixed an ε as the analogy of the first person.
The forms ἐμεῖς, ἐσεῖς and ἐμᾶς, ἐσᾶς are a pluraliza-
tion of ἐμέ and ἐσέ. Since the 6th century the
form σεῖς occurs. The forms ἐμεῖς and ἐσεῖς are
found only since the 16th century. For the genitive
and dative singular one form is used; this is in
the first person μου and in the second σου. Of the
accusative the corresponding forms are με and σε.
In the plural we have μας and σας for both genitive
and accusative. These forms are used also for the
dative.

In the inflection of αὐτός the first syllable is
omitted: (αὐ)τοῦ, (αὐ)τό, etc. In the ancient
Athenian ' tabulæ defixionis ' (formules of exsecra-
tion) we find also the transitory form ἀτός.

Of the *reflexive pronouns* almost the only existing
form is that of the first person: ἐμαυτοῦ. Sometimes
also the form of the third is found. To these are
added the conjunctive forms of the personal
pronoun in the genitive: τοῦ ἐμαυτοῦ μου, τὸν ἐμαυτό
μου, etc. Or: τοῦ ἐμαυτοῦ του (or της), τοῦ ἐμαυτοῦ
μας, τὸν ἐμαυτό μας—τοῦ ἐμαυτου σας, τὸν ἐμαυτό
σας, τοῦ ἐμαυτοῦ τους, τὸν ἐμαυτό τους.

The *possessive pronouns* are μου, σου, του:
τὸ σπίτι μου (from the Latin *hospitium*), τὸ σπίτι
σου, τὸ σπίτι του, τὸ σπίτι μας, τὸ σπίτι σας, etc. =
my house, thy house, his house, our house, your
house. The ancient pronouns ἐμός, σός, etc., are
found only in the Pontic dialect.

The *demonstrative pronouns* are αὐτός, αὐτόνος (genitive αὐτουνοῦ), ἐτοῦτος or τοῦτος (feminine τούτη, genitive τουτουνοῦ), ἐκεῖνος, τέτοιος,[1] τόσος, ὁ ἴδιος = himself.

The *relative pronouns* are replaced by the adverb ποῦ. In the oblique cases του, τον, τῆς, τήν, etc., is added. For example, ἡ ἐφημερὶς, ποῦ τὴν γράφει ὁ Σουρῆς the journal, which Suris writes. Besides ποῦ also ὁ ὁποῖος is used as a relative pronoun.[2]

Interrogative pronouns: τίς (neuter τί). In the plural there is only the form τί; for example, τί ἄντρες εἶναι αὐτοί ; = what sort of men are these ? Also in the singular sometimes τίς is replaced by τί; for example, τί ὥρα εἶναι ; = what o'clock is it ? Besides τίς there is also the pronoun ποjός (ποjά, ποjό) = ancient ποῖος. In the genitive beside ποjοῦ (ποjᾶς) a parallel form occurs : ποιανοῦ (ποιανῆς), an adjective derived from ποῖος.

The *indefinite pronouns:* κανείς (developed from κἂν (= καὶ ἄν) εἷς)[3] or κανένας (κἂν ἕνας) with the feminine καμμια (*κἂνμία) and the neuter κανέν. If a verb with a negative follows, we have also (οὐ) δέν : κανεὶς δὲν ξέρει = nobody knows. ' Something ' is κάτι τι and with a negation—τίποτε = nothing (properly : what at any time ?). ' Some ' is κάτι (indeclinable) or μερικά : κάτι νερό = some

---

[1] From *τοιτοῖος—τοῖος.

[2] ὅποιος signifies ' whosoever '—ὅποιος σὲ ἴδη, θὰ γελάση = whosoever will see thee, will laugh.

[3] Already in the Gospel of St. Luke ii, 72 : κἂν ἐν γὰρ δὴ τοῦτο ἀληθεύων λέγω.

water; κάτι or μερικοὶ στρατιῶτες = some soldiers.
' Somebody ' is κάπojos (from κᾶν ποῖοs). ' Everybody ' is καθείs or καθένας.[1] To the English 'each '
corresponds the indeclinable word κάθε. For
example, κάθε φορὰ = each time. ' Of a certain
size or number ' is κάμποσος (kambossos).

There is no reciprocal pronoun. As in other
languages its place is taken by the expression
' one another '—ὁ ἔνας τὸν ἄλλον—or by the word
ἀναμεταξύ (for example, ἀναμεταξύ μας) or by the
middle form of the verb: δέρνονται = they beat one
another.

Of the *prepositions* the following have new forms
in Modern Greek: 's = εἰs (with the article it
forms one word: στόν, στήν = (εἰ)s τόν, (εἰ)s τήν.
This 's takes also the place of ἐν with the dative:
στὴν πόλιν [2] (= εἰs τὴν πόλιν = ἐν τῇ πόλει). Another
form of εἰs is σέ. The preposition ἐξ has *become* ξε
in compound verbs, because the ε was taken to be
an augment: ξεκινῶ = ἐκκινῶ. The preposition
μετὰ with the genitive has become με with the
accusative and μετὰ with the accusative is replaced
by ὕστερ' ἀπό. The preposition διά is pronounced
γjά and signifies: for, because of, to, about, con-

---

[1] Of καθ'ἔνα—cf. *Papyrus du Louvre*, 62, ii, 6 ; in Spanish
cada uno, and in French *chacun*.

[2] The Turkish name of Constantinople is Stambul from the
Greek στὰν πόλι(ν) = Stamboli. The Dorian form of the
article (τάν) may be explained here by the fact that Byzantium
was actually a Dorian colony. The modern Greeks call this
town simply ἡ πόλις. But Kalinka proposes another explica-
tion of the word Stambul : (κων)σταν (τίνο) πόλι(s). Cf.
Jahrbücher für Altertumswiss., 1920.

cerning. Instead of ἄνευ—χωρίς is used. All the prepositions govern the accusative.

The special forms of the *cardinal numbers* in Modern Greek are:—

1. ἔνας [1] (the accusative of εἷς, which has been made nominative by the ending s. The genitive is ἐνοῦς; the feminine μιά = μία, the neuter ἔνα).
2. δυό (= δύο; cf. μιά).
4. τέσσερις or τέσσεροι = τέσσαρες.
6. ἔξι [2] = ἔξ (pronounce *exi*).
7. ἐφτά = ἐπτά (pronounce *eftá*).
8. ὀχτώ = ὀκτώ.
9. ἐννjά = ἐννέα (from ἐ-νϝα, in Sanscrit *nava*).
11. ἔντεκα = ἔνδεκα (pronounce *endeka*).
13. δεκατρεῖς.
16. δεκάξι = δεκαέξι.
17. δεκαφτά = δεκαεφτά.
18. δεκοχτώ.
19. δεκαννjά.
20. εἴκοσι (ϝι—kṇti—*vimcatis*, Avestan *visaiti*).
30. τριάντα = τριάκοντα (pronounce *trianda*).
40. σαράντα = τεσσαράκοντα (pronounce *saranda*).
50. πενῆντα = πεντήκοντα (pronounce *peninda*).
60. ἐξῆντα = ἐξήκοντα (pronounce *exinda*).
70. ἐβδομῆντα = ἐβδομήκοντα (pronounce *ewdo-minda*).
80. ὀγδῶντα = ὀγδώηκοντα (pronounce *ogdonda*).

---

[1] We find this form already in the 6th century.
[2] Already in the 10th century.

90. ἐνενῆντα (= ἐνενήκοντα).
100. ἑκατό(ν).
700. ἑφτακόσιοι (= ἑπτακόσιοι).
800. ὀχτακόσιοι.
900. ἐννιακόσιοι.
2,000. δυὸ χιλιάδες.
1,000,000. ἔνα ἑκατομμύριο (ἔνα μιλιοῦνι).

The *ordinals* are the same as in Ancient Greek, but the cardinals are often used instead: on the fifteenth of March = 'σταὶς δεκαπέντε Μαρτίου.

The *distributives* are formed from the cardinals with the preposition ἀπό: ἀπὸ εἴκοσι = twenty and twenty.

The *adverbs* of numerals are formed by the substantive φορά prefixed by a numeral: τρεῖς φορές = three times. In multiplication this φορές is omitted: τρεῖς δέκα κάνουν τριάντα.

The multiplicatives have the ending πλός instead of the old πλοῦς (διπλός, τριπλός = διπλοῦς, etc.).

The Modern Greek *verb* has lost many of its ancient parts, but, on the other hand, it has been enriched by many new formations. The verbs in μι have disappeared; there is no middle aorist, no reduplicated perfect, no optative, and no infinitive. The last has been preserved only in some periphrastic forms, and occasionally as a substantive; for example: θὰ ἔχω γράψει(ν) = I will have written; θὰ ἔχει γραφθῆ(ναι) = it will have been written; τὸ φιλεῖ(ν), τὸ φαγεῖ(ν). In general the

I

place of the infinitive has been taken by νὰ (= ἵνα) with the subjunctive.[1]

New forms are: (1) the continual future: θὰ γράφω; (2) the absolute future: θὰ γράψω (θά with the aorist subjunctive); (3) the future perfect: θὰ ἔχω γράψει(ν)[2]; (4) the perfect with the auxiliary verb ἔχω: ἔχω γραμμένο = I have written; (5) the pluperfect: εἶχα γραμμένο[3]; (6) the conditional: θὰ ἔγραφα or ἤθελα γράφει = I would write.

The augment hardly exists except in its syllabic form, and even this is often omitted unless it carries the accent: ἔγραψα, but (ἐ)γράψαμε(ν). A trace of the temporal augment is the fact that in aorist and imperfect indicative the initial ε becomes ει or η: ἔχω, imperfect: εἶχα; εὑρίσκω, aorist: ηὗρα.

Of the participles there remain only the forms γρήφοντας (= γράφων) and (γε)γραμμένος, η, ο.

Only two conjugations are found in Modern Greek: the verbs in ω and the verbs in αω. The old verbs in όω have now the ending όνω or ώνω. This metamorphosis is observed already in the 7th and 8th centuries of our era: κομβώνεις = κομβόω

---

[1] According to Hesseling (*Essai historique sur l'infinitif grec*) from the 12th century the infinitive appears only after few words.

[2] The disappearance of the genuine form of the future was caused by the identity of the form with the subj. aor. Further by the equal pronunciation: παιδεύσεις = παιδεύσῃς, παιδεύσομεν = παιδεύσωμεν.

[3] Thus ἔχω has become an auxiliary, as the correspondent verbs in many modern languages. As such ἔχω appears sometimes already in the antiquity especially in the tragedies. (Cf. Sophocles, *Philoctetes*, v. 1362, σοῦ δ' ἔγωγε θαυμάσας ἔχω; *Antigone*, v. 32, κηρύξαντ' ἔχειν.)

(*Theophanes*, 150, 21), τυφλόνων (ibid., 442, 23), φορτώνω = φορτόω (*Leontius Neapolitanus*, 23, 18). But in some modern dialects (in Cappadokia and on the shores of the Black Sea) the verbs in οω are still preserved: σκοτοῦμαι (not σκοτώνομαι), ὀρθοῦμαι, ἐναντιοῦμαι. As for the verbs in έω, their conjugation is distinguished from the άω-verbs only in the present tense. In the northern dialects even in this tense the verbs on εω are conjugated like those in άω: ἀκολουθᾶς, ὠφελᾶς, πεθυμᾶς (= ἐπιθυμεῖς). On the other hand, in some dialects these verbs have partly preserved their special conjugation in the imperfect: ἐκράτειε (= ἐκράτει), ἐφόριγε (= ἐφόρει-ε + the irrational spirant γ), καρτέριγε (= ἐκαρτερει-ε + γ). Mixed forms also occur: ἐκαρτέριγα (ἐκαρτέρει + the irrational γ + the ending of the conjugation in άω in the third person—αε), ἐφίλιγα (ἐφίλει + γ + α).

Auxiliary verbs in Modern Greek are at present εἶμαι (middle of εἰμί), ἔχω (cf. in vulgar Latin *habeo*, in Italian *avere*, in French *avoir*, in German *haben*, in English ' to have '), and θέλω. In addition the particles θά and ἄς are used in some forms. The former is a mutilated form from θέλω νά. The evolution was as follows: θέλω ἵνα γράψω, θέλω νὰ γράψω, θὲ νὰ γράψω, θὰ νὰ γράψω, θὰν γράψω, and θὰ γράψω.[1] The form θέ instead of θέλει is found for the first time in the 14th century. As for the

---

[1] Cf. Jean Psichari, ' Essai de phonétique néogrecque ' in the *Mémoires de la Société Linguistique*, tome v, Paris, 1884.

assimilation θὲ νὰ to θὰ νὰ, cf. ἀπάνω = ἐπάνω, ἀξαπλωμένος = ἐξαπλωμένος. This θὰ νὰ and θάν occurs for the first time in the 16th century, and in the same century θά we also find.[1]

The particle ἄs is supposed to be an abbreviation of ἄφες (imperative form from ἀφίημι). Indeed, in St. Matthew (xxvii, 49) we read ἄφες ἴδωμεν, which corresponds to the modern ἂς ἰδοῦμεν (let us see !). But Jannaris derives ἄs from ἔασε (imperative from the aorist of ἐάω) ; cf. *Belthandros* : ἔα τὰ περιττὰ καὶ δεῦτε ἂς στραφῶμεν.[2] In Modern Greek we find ἆσε με, ἆς τόν, ἄσ'τούς = let me, let him, let them. The particle is used to form the third person of the imperative ἂs with the subjunctive—ἂs γράφῃ = let him write, ἂς γράφου(ν)ε = let them write. This form of the imperative is found for the first time in *Prodromos*, 3, 269 (12th century).

In the conjugation of the Modern Greek verb contamination has played an important part. The imperfect active has the ending α, not ον by the analogy of the aorist: ἔγραφα = ἔγραφον; ἐπολεμοῦσα: Cauer [2], 301, 4; ἐνίκωσαν, etc. The passive aorist has the ending θηκα, a contamination with the ending of the perfect κα: ἐγράφθηκα = ἐγράφθην. The aorist imperative ends in ε not in ον on the analogy of the present: γράψε = γράψον.[3] Similarly in the passive: γράψου. The imperfect passive ends

---

[1] ἕνα τραγούδι θὰ νὰ πῶ (= θὰ εἴπω)—*Eratokritos*, 83, 6.

[2] Cf. the Byzantine romance *Belthandros*, 184.

[3] Already in antiquity instances of the ending σε instead of σου may be found (cf. Sterret, *An Epigraphical Journey*, i, 82 : δρᾶσε).

in ουν on the analogy of the imperfect active of the verbs in έω (ἐβοήθουν) : ἐγράφομουν = ἐγραφόμην. The persons are : ἐγράφομουν, ἐγράφουσουν, ἐγράφουνταν, ἐγραφούμαστε, ἐγραφούσασθε, ἐγράφουνταν.

The thematic vowel in the subjunctive is short (not long) on the analogy of the indicative: νὰ γράφετε = ἵνα γράφητε.

The auxiliary εἶμαι is held to be a middle formed from εἰμί and is conjugated in the following manner: εἶμαι, εἶσαι, εἶναι (sometimes wrongly written εἶνε), εἴμαστε (in vulgar Greek εἴμεθα cf. Migne, *Patrologia græca*, t. 87, p. 3096), εἶστε, εἶναι. Imperfect: ἤμουν by analogy of the imperfect of the verbs in έω: ἐβοήθουν; in vulgar Greek ἤμην, ἤσουν, ἦταν(ε) (in vulgar Greek ἦτο), ἤμαστε, ἤσαστε, ἦταν(ε). Already in antiquity sometimes instead of ἐστί or ἔνεστι, we meet the preposition ἔνι (= ἐν). Cf. Homer, the tragedians and the sentence ἐγγύα, παρὰδ' ἄτα, where similarly the preposition παρά seems to be the predicate. Further, cf. the inscription on a Corinthian cup of the 6th century before Christ: καλὸ ἔνι τὸ ποτήριον (Pottier, *Vases antiques du Louvre*, 2me série, p. 97) and St. Paul, Gal. iii, 28: οὐκ ἔνι Ἰουδαῖος οὐδὲ Ἕλλην (similarly, Col. iii, 11—οὐκ ἔνι Ἕλλην καὶ Ἰουδαῖος). The fact that the preposition seems to have become predicate may be easily explained by an ellipse of the verb: ἐν (ἐστί) has become ἔνι, like παρά (εστι)—παρά. Finally, ἔνι has become εἶναι on the analogy of the first person εἶμαι (= εἰμί).

The Modern Literary Language

We have said that by the side of the living language of conversation (called ἡ δημώδης or ἡ χυδαία γλῶσσα) about 1700 a peculiar literary language was developed called ἡ γραπτὴ γλῶσσα or ἡ καθαρεύουσα. It is called ' pure ' language, because those who use it are endeavouring to remove all elements by which the living language differs from the old κοινή. At the same time, words for modern ideas, which the δημώδης borrows immediately from the foreign languages, in the καθαρεύουσα are translated into genuine Greek. We will mention here the most important peculiarities of this form of the language, which in Modern Greek is official.

A. *The Vocabulary.*—(1) Instead of new words which have appeared in the language of conversation, the old ones are revived. For example, οἶνος instead of κρασί (formed in the δημώδης from the old word κρᾶσις = mixture; in antiquity wine was usually drunk mixed with water), ἄρτος instead of ψωμί (= the old word ψωμίον—crumb). But old words thus revived have now sometimes a new meaning : ἀφιππεύω (instead of ξεπεζεύω of the living language) = to dismount; the old signification was : to ride away. (2) As already mentioned, new words are formed on the basis of ancient Greek, for example, ἀνελκυστήρ = lift, ποδελάτης = bicycle. Since about 1750, according to the testimony of the learned

Kumanudis, the language has been thus enriched by nearly 60,000 new words (cf. Hatzidakis, Γλωσσολογικαὶ μελέται, p. 271). (3) But also foreign words were directly borrowed; for example, ἀπαρθενεύω = the French *appartenir*.

B. *The Grammar*.—An endeavour is made to follow the ancient system of declension and conjugation. But of the old forms the following are excluded: (1) the infinitive, the place of which is taken by νά with the subjunctive; (2) the dual; (3) the optative; (4) the future, for which with the subjunctive is used, and (5) the second aorist.

In syntax and in the turn of phrases much confusion prevails, owing to the practice of translating French and German expressions directly into Greek. In *belles lettres* French expressions are most commonly used; in scientific books this place is taken by German. Finally, it must be observed that the standard of the καθαρεύουσα varies a good deal from one author to another [1]; this is because of the absence of definite rules to govern usage.

The style of modern authors fluctuates between the forms of language: the Ancient Greek and the Vulgar Greek, sometimes approaching to the one and sometimes to the other. Psicharis, one of the

---

[1] One must not suppose that everything is to-day written in Greece in the καθαρεύουσα. There are many renowned authors who exclusively write in the language of conversation. Others sometimes use one, sometimes the other. Cf. E. Brighenti, *Crestomazia Neoellenica*, Milano, 1908, and Pernot et Legrand, *Chrestomathie grecque moderne*, 1899.

most energetic champions of the introduction of
the pure vulgar language into literature, remarks
that no two authors write the same καθαρεύουσα,
and that everyone writes his own language (cf. the
journal Ἄστυ of May 18, 1900). Also a chronological difference has been observed in this language.
Rhoïdis testifies that it is changing every year
(cf. Εἴδωλα, p. 374). Hatzidakis distinguishes three
forms of the καθαρεύουσα : (1) the rigid type
(ἡ αὐστηρὰ καθαρεύουσα), a language closely approaching to Ancient Greek or the κοινή, written, for
example, by Alexander Rhangavis; (2) the moderate
type (ἡ ἀνειμένη κ.) such as that of Emmanuel
Rhoïdis or the historian Paparrhigopoulos; and
(3) that vulgar type (ἡ δημοδεστέρα) written, for
example, by Damverghis, Drosinis, and other
novelists. His opinion is that the latter form will
in the end prevail, and that in this form the
language of conversation and the literary language
will be fixed into one unity.

Chapter VII

THE MODERN GREEK DIALECTS

We have already observed that although the Ancient Greek dialects disappeared in the course of the first two centuries of our era,[1] the language has not been truly rendered uniform; on the basis of that common form of Greek called the κοινή a fresh set of dialects arose in the various parts of the Greek world, and these may be regarded as the ancestors of the dialects of the contemporary language.

We must observe that these dialects differ one from another not so much in their morphology as in their phonetics. From the point of view of phonetics two great groups of dialects may be distinguished: a northern and a southern group. To the former belong Thrace, Macedonia, Thessaly, and the northern islands; to the other the southern regions and islands. According to Hatzidakis the line of separation between these two groups is the 38th degree of northern latitude. Further, also a western and an eastern group may be distinguished.

[1] According to A. Thumb; Hatzidakis thinks during the first four centuries, and W. Schmid in the 5th century. (Cf. *Wochenschrift für klass. Philologie*, 1901, col. 564.)

To the western belong the regions and islands named above; to the eastern the eastern islands: Chios (Skió), Naxos (Antiparo), Paros, Rhodes, Cyprus, and the continent of Asia Minor. In the north, for example, *E* without an accent becomes an *I*, and *O* becomes an unaccented *U*. *I* and *U* without an accent disappear totally (except in the last syllable of a word). For example, ἀγοράζω (I buy) becomes ἀγουράζου; ἔστειλε (pronounce *estile*) becomes ἔστλι; δουλεύει (*dulevi* = he works)— δλέβ (*dlev*); ψυχή becomes ψή, etc. Of the eastern dialects the characteristic mark is the preservation of *v* in the ending of a substantive: τὸν ἀδελφόν, not τὸν ἀδελφό or ἀδερφό. The χ is pronounced before *I* and *E* as *sh*. Instead of χέρι (= χέριον = χεῖρ) *sheri* is used; instead of ἔχει (= *ekhi*)—*eshi*.

In general in Modern Greek eight dialects may be distinguished,[1] although many sub-varieties are also to be distinguished. These eight main dialects are as follows: (1) the continent of Greece (with the exception of Thessaly) and Eubœa, Ægina and the Ionian islands; (2) Thrace, Macedonia, and Thessaly; (3) the northern islands; (4) the south-eastern islands; (5) Crete, the Cyclades, and the Sporades; (6) Cyprus; (7) Asia Minor; and (8) the Greek dialects of Southern Italy.

In the dialects of the continental Greece with the neighbouring islands and in Italy (dialects 1, 2, and

---

[1] Interesting examples of the dialects of Modern Greece may be found in the play of Visantios—Βαβυλωνία.

8) we find a very interesting apparent archaism: non-contracted forms of the verbs in άω : (ἐ)ρωτάω (instead of ῥωτῶ), ῥωτάεις, ῥωτάει, ἐρώταες, ἐρώταε, ἐρωτάαμε, ἐρώτααν. But these forms are not genuine archaisms, and in fact are found only from the 16th century onwards. They are the result of a contamination of the second person ἐρωτᾶς, ἐρωτᾶτε with the usual forms on εις, ετε, etc.

The non-contracted forms πατειοῦμαι (from πατέομαι), πατειέσαι, πατειέται, πατειούμεσθα, etc., which occur from the 12th century, seem to be the result a soft pronunciation of the consonant *t* before vowels. The sound has become a *tj* (τ = τj; ει = I).[1]

The principal features of the different groups of the dialects are the following:—

THE FIRST GROUP

(The mainland of Greece, Eubœa, Ægina, and the Ionian Islands)

Phonetics

(*a*) In the endings έο, έα, ίο, ία, the accented vowel is preserved and has not become a *j*, as usually (except Pontos, Asia Minor, and Southern Italy) : παιδία, μηλέα (not παιδjά, μηλjά).

---

[1] Such a softening of consonants is well known in Slavonic languages.

(b) In the Maïna the sound I develops another I in the preceding syllable: βájζει (*vaisi*) instead of βáζει (*vasi*).

(c) In the same territory γ = j becomes ž (= the French j): ζῆ (ži = ji) instead of γη, μαζεριτσή (*majeritsi*) = μαγερική.

(d) In Athens, Ægina, Megara, and Eubœa υ and sometimes οι are pronounced as U: στσοῦλος = σκῦλος (*shtshulos*), τσουλία = κοιλιά, σčοῦνι = σχοινίον, κšοῦλα = ξύλα, čούτη = κοίτη.

Morphology

(a) Instead of the aorist formed with σ we have an aorist formed with κ by analogy with the perfect: ἄκουκα = ἤκουσα, ἐχτύπηκα = ἐχτύπησα.

(b) The old ending ουσι of the third person plural present still exists in Maïna, while elsewhere it is replaced by ουν.

(c) In Ægina the aorist passive has the ending θηνα instead of θηκα: ἐδέθηνα = ἐδέθηκα.

(d) In addition to the preposition ἐκ, we have in this group also ὀχ (ὀχ τὸν πόλεμον = ἐκ τοῦ πολέμου = because of the war).

THE SECOND GROUP

(Thrace, Macedonia, Thessaly)

Phonetics

(a) The vowel O becomes an U (cf. the old Æolian dialects).

(*b*) After π and τ the consonant ι becomes χî :
κουμματχîα = κομμάτια.

(*c*) After φ, θ, and σ the same consonant becomes
κj : χουράφκja = χωράφια (χωράφι = acre).

(*d*) Between vowels the consonant σ falls out,
if the following syllable ends with *s*: νὰ φκειάης =
νὰ φκειάσης (that thou dost).

(*e*) In the imperfect and the aorist the accent
of the singular is preserved also in the plural:
ἔρχουμουν—ἔρχουμὰστουν.

Morphology

(*a*) The article is *i* instead of ό: *i* ἄνθρωπος (so
too in Lesbos).

(*b*) The nominative plural is used also for the
accusative (also in Asia Minor).

(*c*) Instead of ποῖος, we find τούλογος or τίλογος =
τιλογῆς = of what sort ?

The Third Group

(The Northern Islands)

Phonetics

Before *I* τ becomes κ: αὐκί (= αὐτί = ear),
(μάκι = eye, from μάτι).

Morphology

(*a*) The interrogative pronoun is τίδα (= τίντα)
or ἴντα.

(*b*) The imperative of the passive has the ending
τσι instead of σου: δράπτσι = ντράψου (from ἐντ-
ρέπομαι).

(*c*) The diminutives have the ending ελ (= ελλ):
κερατέλ (from κέρατο).[1]

THE FOURTH GROUP
(The South-eastern Islands)

Phonetics

(*a*) *j* after an unvoiced consonant becomes σ
or *sh*. After a voiced consonant it becomes ζ or *ž*:
πσός or πšός = ποjός, αὔρžο = αὔρjο = αὔριον.

(*b*) In some islands σσ becomes τσ and ζ (= *z* = *s*
in the German *so*)—*ds*: γλῶτσα (= γλῶσσα),
παίδζω (= παίζω).

(*c*) The ending εύω of the verbs becomes εύγω:
πιστεύγω = πιστεύω. Naturally βω becomes βγω,
for *v* and β sound alike.

Morphology

The interrogative pronoun is ἴντα (cf. groups
3 and 6).

THE FIFTH GROUP
(Crete and the Cyclades)

Phonetics

(*a*) μπ, γκ, ντ are = *b*, *g*, *d*—not *mb*, *ng*, *nd*:
μπορῶ = *boró* = εἰμπορῶ = I can; φεγγάρι = *fegari*
= the moon; κοντά = *kodá* = near.

---

[1] Cf. κερατάς = the devil (in Russian *čert* = *čort*).

Morphology

(a) ὁ βασιλές = βασιλιάς (= βασιλέας).

(b) Augment is η instead of ε: ἤκαμα (= ἔκαμα from κάμνω = I do), ἤφνα = ἔφυγα.

(c) Instead of ἐρωτοῦσα (imperfect of ἐρωτάω)— ἐρώτουν (ἐρώτας, ἐρώτα, etc.). Instead of ἐπατοῦσα (imperfect of πατέω)—ἐπάτεja (ἐπάτεjας, ἐπάτειε).

THE SIXTH GROUP
(Cyprus)

Phonetics

(a) β, γ, and δ between vowels disappear: κάουρας (= κάβουρας = crab), συλλοῦμαι (= συλλογοῦμαι), ἀερφός (= ἀδερφός = ἀδελφος).

(b) ρχ becomes ρκ: ἔρκουμαι = ἔρχομαι.

(c) Instead of κκ, ππ, and ττ we have the aspirants κh, πh, and τh: πίτhα = πίττα or πίσσα, λάκhος = λάκκος.

(d) βγ, βδ, and γδ become βκ, βτ, and γτ: ἐβτομάδα = ἐβδομάδα = week; βκαίννω = βγαίννω = βαίνω.

(e) j after a consonant becomes κj: χαρκjά = χαρτjά = cards,—or κ: χωρκό(ν) = χωρjό(ν) = χωρίον.

Morphology

(a) ἐγjῶ or ἐγjώνη = ἐγώ.

(b) The aorist imperative passive has the ending θου instead of σου: λυπήθου = λυπήσου.

(c) The future is formed with ἐννά instead of θά.

THE SEVENTH GROUP
(Asia Minor [1])

Phonetics

(a) η is sometimes pronounced as ε : ἐφέκα = ἀφῆκα.

(b) The syllables *ja* and *jo* or *vo* are pronounced as *ae* and *oe* in Latin : λοένω = λυώνω = λύω.

(c) στ becomes σσ: σσό = στό = 's τό = εἰs τό.

Morphology

(a) The possessive pronouns ἐμός and ἐμέτερος = ἡμέτερος (η = e) are preserved (instead of μου and μαs).

(b) Instead of τί—ντό. Instead of τό—ἀ. Instead of αὐτός—ἄτs (τὸν υἱονάτ = τὸν υἱὸν αὐτοῦ). Instead of του—ἄχτέ(s). Instead of οὗτος—ἀβοῦτος.

(c) Neuter instead of masculine : ὁ φίλον = ὁ φίλος (plural : οἱ φίλjα = οἱ φίλοι, τῶν φιλjῶν, etc.).

(d) Instead of the ending ίζομαι—ίσκουμαι : ταγίσκουμαι = ταγίζομαι.

(e) Aorists : ἐποῖκα (= Ancient Greek πεποίηκα), ἐσέγκα (= Ancient Greek εἰσήνεγκα), ἐξέγκα (= old ἐξήνεγκα).

(f) ἔν = (ἔν)εστι.

(g) The old infinitive is preserved in the regions on the shore of the Black Sea. Similarly the verbs on όω and the imperative of the aorist on ον : κούρευσον, κάψον.

---

[1] Cf. R. Dawkins, *Modern Greek in Asia Minor*, Cambridge, 1910.

(*h*) The negation instead of ὄχι (from οὐχί) is κί (= οὐκί). In Cappadokia we meet also the old forms ἦσαν and ἐστέ. The third person of the plural is ἔνται (= εἰσί).

THE EIGHTH GROUP

Southern Italy (Terra d'Otranto and Bova) [1]

Phonetics

(*a*) γ is pronounced before dump vowels as *g*, not as *gh*.

(*b*) λ between vowels becomes *ḍḍ* (*d* spoken with the top of the tongue bent backwards): *puḍḍi* = πουλί (= the bird).

(*c*) The ς in the ending is suppressed: *jeláï* = γελάεις.

(*d*) In the Terra d'Otranto θ beginning a word is pronounced *t*; internally it becomes a *s*: *teó* = θεός, *lisari* = λιθάρι.

(*e*) δ is pronounced as *d*, not *ds*.

(*f*) χτ becomes φτ: *niftá* = νύχτα.

(*g*) In Bova both χτ and φτ become στ: *nista* (= νύχτα); *está* = ἐφτά.

(*h*) ξ and ψ are pronounced in the Terra d'Otranto as *fs*: *afsiló* (= ὑψηλός), *fsero* (= ξέρω = εἰξεύρω = οἶδα).

(*i*) ξ and ψ in Bova become *dz*: *dzilo* (ξύλο), *dzomi* (= ψωμί = ψωμίον).

[1] Cf. Morosi, *I dialetti greci della terra d'Otranto*, 1870.

Morphology

(a) The indefinite article is *a* instead of ἕνας:
a sacco = ἕνα σάκκο.

(b) The *s* and *n* in the endings of the sub-stantives in general disappear.

(c) The substantives in *as* have in the plural the ending *i*: *andras* (= ἄντρας = ἀνήρ)—*andri*.

(d) Instead of μjά—*ma*: *ma ghineka* = μjά γυναῖκα (= γυνή).

(e) Instead of ἐγώ (*eghó*)—*evó*; theγ has been replaced by *v*.

(f) Instead of τις—*tio* (accus. *tino* or *tio*).

(g) *Cispu* = ὅστις, *passo* = πᾶς (neuter *passio*, femin. *passia*), *puti* = ὅτι.

(h) *Peo, pea, pei* = ποῖος.[1]

[1] According to the usual explanation the Greeks of southern Italy are the descendants of colonists who came to Italy in the Middle Ages. But Gerhard Rohlfs in *Griechen und Romanen in Unteritalien* (Geneva, 1924) thinks that they are descendants of *old* Greek colonists. Indeed, we know Greek inscriptions of the 6th century at Naples, and southern Italy was under Byzantine sway till the 9th century, when Greek colonists came again from Greece.

APPENDIX

I

A SURVEY OF THE HISTORY OF PHONETICS IN GREEK

The sounds which form the words of a language are changing in the course of time generally according to some rules.[1] But these rules have exceptions due to the influence of analogy, assimilation, and dissimilation. Each change, qualitative or quantitative, occurs under certain circumstances. The principal rules of the Greek phonetics are the following:—

1. A general phenomenon in the language is the so-called—by a German word—*Ablaut*, i.e. the regular change of the vowel of the root or of the suffix of a word. There are three degrees of the *Ablaut*: the full, the middle or the reduced, and the feeble grade. According to Hirt (*Griechische Laut- und Formenlehre*, p. 147) we have in Greek the following cases: (1) Roots with a long vowel $\bar{o}$:

---

[1] Some philologists speak of 'laws' of the change of sounds; but the 'laws' cannot admit exceptions. Brugmann and the so-called 'Young Grammarians' (*Junggrammatiker*), indeed, assert that the laws of the phonetics have no exceptions. This opinion is given up by most philologers. Cf. Havet in *Bull. de la Société Linguistique*, xvi (1910), p. 44.

ō—ē—a (e): θω—μός, τί—θη—μι, τι—θε—μεν. (2)
Roots with a short vowel o: o—e—O: ὄχος—ἔχω—
ἔσχον =*séσεχον. (3) Roots with the sound u: ὔοι—
ὔει—u, or οὔ—εὔ—ŭ: ἐλή—λου—θα, ἐ—λεύ—σομαι,
ἤλυθον; ἄ—Fοι—δός, ἀ—Fέι—δω, ἀ—ύ—δη. (4)
Roots with the sound i: oi—ei—i: στοῖχος, στεῖχω,
στίχος.

2. The semi-vowel i of the primitive language
became in Greek at the beginning of words a
spiritus asper (ὅς, cf. in Sanscrit yas) or ζ (ζυγόν,
cf. in Latin iugum). Sommer explains this difference
in the following manner: the sound i became a ζ:
(1) if the next syllable contained a s or a h (ζώννυμι
from *ζώσνυμι, cf. iungo). As the sound s often
became in Greek a ρ (rhotacism), i became a ζ
also before ρ + a consonant (ζόρξ, cf. in Russian
júrkij = alert). (2) before v = u: ζυγόν. In the
middle of words the i disappeared between two
vowels: τιμάω from *τιμάιω (cf. in Latin the ending
io of verbs (ex. gr. munio) and in Russian:
čitáiu = I read). In the Homeric form κείαται the i
is preserved by analogy with κεῖμαι. Homer has
preserved i in certain formulæ: ἴως (ὥς), if this
word is postponed (ὄρνιθες ἰώς—Iliad, iii, 2—or
πέλεκυς ἰώς—iii, 60).

3. The digamma (F) became in the text of
Homer and sometimes elsewhere after a vowel a v,
so that a diphthong was formed: εὔιδον = *ἐ-Fιδον,
cf. in Sanscrit a-vidam; κεραυνός from κεραFνός.

4. Generally the digamma disappeared without

leaving change, first between vowels, then at the beginning of words. Its existence is proved: (1) by comparative philology (εἶδον from *ἔ-Ϝιδον, because in Latin we find *video*, in Russian *vídjetj*); (2) by the fact that some verbs beginning with a vowel have nevertheless the syllabic augment ἑάλων = *ἐϜάλων, from Ϝαλίσκομαι; (3) by the fact that contraction is omitted: ἑορτή (not *ὠρτή), from ϜεϜορτή, ἕως (from *ἦϜος, cf. in Sanscrit *javat*), πλέομεν (from πλέϜομεν, cf. in Slavonian *plyvémy*); (4) by the fact that the privative particle is α, not αν: ἄεργος (from ἀ-Ϝεργος and Ϝέργον; if ἔργον were primitive, we would find *ἄνεργος), ἀ-ίδηλος (from ἀϜίδηλος; stem is Ϝιδ).

As we see, the digamma at the beginning of words is sometimes replaced by the spiritus asper. It sounded like the English *wh* in ' wheel': ἔρση from Ϝέρση (cf. in Sanscrit *varšam* = the rain).

Between vowels the Ϝ disappeared and before ρ it was assimilated to this consonant: ἄρρητος = *ἄ-Ϝρητος. In Lesbian and Bœotian Ϝ at the beginning of words before ρ became a β: βρήτωρ = Ϝρήτωρ = ῥήτωρ (cf. in Latin *orator*, in Russian *orátj* = to roar).

If the Ϝ disappeared after consonants, the preceding vowel was lengthened: ξεῖνος (pron. *ksénos*) instead of *ξένϜος (ει expresses a long ε), οὖλος instead of *ὄλϜος (cf. in Sanskrit *sárvas*). In Attic the vowel was not lengthened: ξένος, κόρη (from *κόρϜη—*κόρϜα; cf. in Russian, *Kúrva* =

πόρνη). In Lesbian the consonant was doubled, while the vowel remained unaffected: ξέννος.

A dental + Ϝ became in Greek a θ: in Slavonic, zvérj; in Greek, θήρ.

5. The sibilant σ at the beginning of words before vowels usually became a spiritus asper: ἵστημι, cf. in Latin sisto; ἔξ (from *sϜέξ); cf. in Latin sex; ἅλς, cf. in Latin sal; ἕπομαι, cf. sequor, etc. When the s has disappeared without leaving a trace, we must suppose the influence of analogy or a dissimilation of aspirates: ἀπατούρια (from *ἀπατούρια = sm̥—πατούρια; cf. in Latin simul), ἔχω (from *ἔχω, cf. ἕξω). Between vowels in the middle of a word the s also became an h, but later the sound disappeared completely (cf. the j and the Ϝ), or, if it stood in the second syllable, the spiritus was removed over to the beginning of the first: γένους (from *γένεσος), μυός (from *μυσός; cf. in Slavonic myš, in German Maus, in English ' mouse '), ἱερός (cf. in Sanscrit iširah), ἕως (from ἠώς, cf. in Sanscrit uṣāh).

6. Vowels before vowels are shortened: βασιλέων (from *βασιλήων), ἕως (from ἠώς).

7. In Ionic and Attic adjacent vowels exchange quantity; this is called the metathesis of quantity: βασιλέως (from βασίληος; so actually in Lesbian), Δεινοδίκεω (from Δεινοδίκηο; cf. Cauer, Delectus inscriptionum[2], 516), πόλεως (cf. πόληος in Homer), εθντεῶτος; cf. θνητός.

8. Two adjacent vowels, if the word contains

more than one syllable, and if no other has fallen
out between the vowels, form one sound: φιλεῖτε [1]
(from φιλέετε; the ει is a lengthened ē), τιμᾶτε (from
τιμάετε). A diphthong may originate, if the second
vowel is a υ or an ι: πάϊς—παῖς, βέλεϋς (*βέλεσος)—
βέλευς.

9. The sonant nasals of Indo-German m̥ and n̥
appear in Greek as a or αν (before vowels and if the
nasal was accented): δέκα (from *δέκm̥t; cf. in
Latin decem and in Slavonic desn̥tj), τέκταινα
(from *τέκτανja and *τεκτn̥ja), ἔασι (in Ionian
εἰσί) from *ἔσαντι, in Indo-Germanic sn̥ti, in
Sanscrit sánti.

10. The sonant liquids r̥ and l̥ became in Greek
ρα and λα or αρ and αλ. This variation is explained
by Kretschmer (Kuhns Zeitschrift, 31, 391) and
Hirt (Indogermanische Forschungen, 7, 138). The
latter regards αρ and αλ as anomaly partly on
the analogy of forms containing ερ: σπείρω,
σπαρτός, or to have originated under the influence of
metric: θαρσαλέος in Homer beside θρασυκάρδιος,
or to be dialectical forms, or finally to be ₑr,
i.e. r preceded by a whispered vowel e.

11. A long vowel was usually shortened before
ῐ or ῠ + nasal, a sibilant or a liquid (a rule discerned
by Osthoff): Ζεύς from *Ζήνς (cf. in Sanscrit
Djāus), νᾰῦς from *νᾱῦς (cf. the Ionic νηῦς). By this
rule we may also explain the fact that the augment

---

[1] In modern Greek ε appears after ει: φιλεῖεται, as the
analogy of κυλίεται; cf. ἐκράτειε, ἐκάλειε.

is not formed in verbs beginning with a diphthong: εὔξατο. If nevertheless ηὔξατο is found also, it must be regarded as a later formation, perhaps on the analogy of ἦγον.

12. Before ρ in the beginning of words and later before σ + a consonant an ε has originated, and before a dental an ο—the so-called ' prothesis ': ἐ-ρυθρός; cf. in Sanscrit *rudhiráh*, in Latin *ruber*, in Russian *rúsyj*. In general no Greek word could begin with a ρ; if this occurs sometimes we must suppose the loss of a consonant or a semi-vowel before this sound: ῥήτωρ, from *Ϝρήτωρ; ῥήτρα, from Ϝράτρα (in Eleian inscriptions we find actually this word); ῥίγος, from *Ϝρίγος (in Latin *frigus*). The prothesis occurs also before other consonants, but in this case we must suppose an ' Ablaut ' or an epic lengthening or that the prothetic vowel represents a preposition or a whispered sound: ἐ-χθές, from ₑχθες; ἴσθι, from ₑσθι (the root is *es*). Also in Modern Greek the prothesis occurs sometimes: ἀ-χείλι = χείλι = χεῖλος; ἀ-μολύνω instead of μολύνω; ἀ-τσιγγάνι instead of τσιγγάνι (=a gipsy).

13. Between two consonants (especially liquids or nasals) a vowel has sometimes been inserted— ' anaptyxis ': ἀλεγεινός = ἀλγεινός (from ἄλγος), ἕβδομος (from *sέπτμος).

14. Between *m* and *r* or *l* a β has originated (' anaptyxis of a consonant ' because a sound had disappeared): μεσημβρία (from *μεσημₑρία), βροτός (from *μροτός and *μβροτός; cf. in Latin

mortalis). Between ν and ρ a δ has appeared: ἀνδρός from *ἀνερός and *ἀνρός.

15. Before a dental or a *s* the ν disappears. The preceding vowel is lengthened (ε—ει = ē̆; o—ου): εἰς from *ἐνς, ὀδοῦσι from *ὀ-δόντσι (cf. in Latin *dent-s*). But this rule is not valued in all dialects.

16. Of two aspirates in adjacent syllables the first becomes a tenuis (dissimilation): τριχός instead of *θριχός (from θρίξ), ταχύς (instead of *θαχύς, cf. θάσσων from *θάγχjων); τίθημι (instead of *θίθημι). In some cases the second aspirate becomes a tenuis: σώθητι instead of *σώθηθι.

17. A Greek word can have no other ending but a vowel or ν, *s*, and ρ.

18. To the gutturals *k* and *gh* with a following *j* (*y*) of the primitive language corresponds in Greek ππ and ττ or σσ: in Sanscrit *pacyati*, in Russian *pecj* (first person of the present: *pekú*), the primitive form *peqjo, in Greek πέσσω (or πέπτω); in Sanscrit *laghu*, in Greek ἐ-λάσσων (from *ἐ-λάghjων).

19. In Greek *dh* + *j* of the primitive language becomes τσ or σσ: in Sanscrit *madhya*, in Greek μεσσος (from *μεδhjos, cf. in Latin *medius*).

20. Before μ the labials are assimilated: ὄπ-μα (cf. ὄπ-ωπ-α) becomes ὄμμα.

21. The dentals (δ, τ, θ) before σ themselves become also σ, and the same thing happens before other dentals: *ἐλπίδς—ἐλπίς, *Ϝοίδ-θα—Ϝοῖσθα.

PART II

AN HISTORICAL SURVEY OF GREEK SYNTAX

Chapter I

GENERALITIES, SUBJECT AND PREDICATE

The word σύνταξις in its usual grammatical signification was used for the first time by Apollonius Dyscolus in the 2nd century of our era in his treatise περὶ συντάξεως. Formerly the old grammarians understood by this word a simple juxtaposition of words, παράθεσις, as opposed to σύνθεσις, which signified the compounding of words; cf. σὺν βίῳ and σύμβιος. But some questions of syntax had been already before that time treated by Protagoras, Aristotle, the Stoics, etc. Apollonius was nevertheless the founder of syntax as a systematic science.

It is well known that syntax deals with the forms of words in clauses, of the nature of clauses in general, and of their union. But what is a clause ? Dionysius the Thracian in the 1st century before Christ defined speech as a joining together of words to express a complete (αὐτοτελής) sentence. But there are clauses which do not express a sentence, but only a feeling, a desire, a command, or an exclamation. In modern times the German philologist Paul has proposed the following definition: the clause is a manifestation of the fact that several

157

ideas have become united in the mind of the speaker and the instrument to produce these same ideas in the mind of the hearer. The objection has been made that this definition would include as clauses also such groups of words as ' the good man.' Paul has replied (in his *Prinzipien der Sprachgeschichte*, p. 123) that such juxtapositions have indeed developed of clauses: ' the good man ' from ' the man is good.'—Wilhelm Wundt defines: ' The clause is an expression in speech of the arbitrary breaking of a general idea into its parts put in logical connexion one with the other.' But a general idea consisting of different parts can be expressed also by a single word: τρίπους, ἄρο-τρον. Consequently Wundt grants that there is no absolute difference between word and clause. For instance, the Latin vocative *Marce !* can be considered as a single word, but also as a clause. The Sanscrit grammarians, therefore, laid it down that there are not only verbal clauses in which the predicate is a verb, but also nominal clauses.[1] We may mention the definition of Paul Kretschmer : ' The clause is a grammatical expression directly produced by feeling or wish.' In this case every interjection would be a clause. Meillet defines the clause from a purely grammatical point of view : ' La phrase est un ensemble d'articulations liées

---

[1] Indeed, in the native language of the Indian grammarians, the Sanscrit, compounds are formed easily so that a clause can be expressed by a single word : *asthibhūjas* = ' who has nothing but his bones.'

entre elles par des rapports grammaticaux, et qui ne dépendent grammaticalement d'aucun autre ensemble et se suffisent à elles mêmes' (cf. his *Introduction*, p. 339).

An essential point in a clause is the presence of the predicate. It is true that there are apparently clauses not having a predicate or a subject. In Greek, in Latin, and in the Slavonic languages the personal pronoun as a subject is often omitted. In Greek and Latin even regularly, if there is no stress on the pronoun. The subject is also, it appears, omitted in such impersonal expressions as βρέχει— it rains, or *ningit*—it snows. But the subject is only seemingly absent. Indeed, ' something ' must be the cause of the rain or of the snow! Further, in Greek from the time of Homer we find clauses which apparently have no predicate, like the well-known οὐκ ἀγαθὸν (ἐστί) πολυκοιρανίη, or οἰωνοὶ δὲ περὶ πλέες (εἰσί) ἠὲ γυναῖκες. Cf. also the inscription *IGA*. 581, A 6: ὅση τῶν οὔρων τούτων ἔσω, πᾶσα Δοφῖτις. That is a use surviving from the times when there was no flexion at all. In Greek and Latin the copula as the predicate is absent in the third person, while in Lithuanian and Russian it is absent also in the first and second person. In Modern Greek, on the contrary, the copula is never absent.

It is natural that the subject should occupy the first place in the clause. Where was the predicate to be placed in the enlarged clause (by an object, an apposition, etc.) ? In Greek and Latin it was put at the end of the principal clause. In subordinate clauses the predicate was put in the middle. This was the case also in Sanscrit. It was for the reason that the verbs (the predicate is a verb) in Sanscrit and in Greek originally were all enclitic,[1] for the beginning of the clause was naturally spoken in a higher key. In the principal clauses the predicate being at the end was spoken with the least emphasis, and therefore as a verb losing its accent. But it is the opinion of many prominent philologists, as Delbrueck and Wackernagel, that this was originally the case in all Indo-European languages. If even in very old inscriptions the verb is not put at the end, this is because in long clauses an effort was made to secure greater clearness by putting the predicate nearer the subject.

It is well known that the predicate must agree with the subject in number, gender, and case. In Ancient Greek we observe an apparent exception from this rule, if the subject is a neuter plural. The predicate is then not in plural, but in singular. But already in Homer we find many exceptions. We find the predicate in plural after such subjects: ἄγγεα, δέρματα, ἕρπετα, λέπαδνα, μέλεα, ὅπλα, οὔθατα, οὖρα, πέδιλα, πτερά, στόματα, τέκνα, φάσγανα, φρείατα, φῦλα, χείλεα, χερμάδια. After other subjects

---

[1] Thence the rule that the accent in the verb is as far as possible drawn back, so that in compounds the verb loses the accent altogether and is placed on the preposition : σύμφερε, κατάκειται.

the usage varies. In the classical period the predicate
was in the neuter plural, when the subject was a
neuter plural, if single objects were in question.
For instance, we read in Xenophon (*Anab.* i, 8):
φανερὰ ἦσαν ἴχνη πολλά. If the plural of the subject
has properly the signification of a singular, as
γοῦνα, μῆρα, ὀστέα being parts of one body, ἄστρα =
the sky, or ὄρεα = a chain of mountains, already
in the Homeric poems the predicate is in the
singular. We find the same thing in the oldest
Sanscrit. In Modern Greek this peculiarity is not
found. Johann Schmidt (in *Die Pluralbildung der
indogermanischen Neutra*, Weimar, 1889) has proposed the explanation that the neuter plural forms
in α were originally in the Indo-European primitive
language singular forms signifying collectives. But
we observe in Greek as also in Latin the contrary
phenomenon, that the predicate is a plural, while
the subject is a singular collective: τὸ πλῆθος
ἐψηφίσαντο πολεμεῖν (*Thucydides*, i, 125), magna
multitudo hominum convenerant. In Latin and in.
Greek the predicate is also a plural, if the subject
is an indefinite pronoun in singular: missi sunt
honoratissimus quisque e patribus (*Livius*, ii, 15),
οὐδεὶς ἐκοιμήθη τοὺς ἀπολωλότας πενθοῦντες (*Xenoph.
Hell.* 2, 2, 3). If the subject is a dual, the predicate
is sometimes already in Homer in the plural:
δεινὼ δέ οἱ ὄσσε φάανθεν.[1] This was so also in Avesta,

---

[1] Also the adjective belonging to a dual substantive is sometimes in the plural: φίλας χεῖρε (*Odyss.*, 11, 211). The cause
was that the dual began already to grow obsolete.

while in Sanscrit the predicate is in such cases also a dual. In Avesta and in Greek we observe also that if the dual subject signifies objects belonging to one another, the predicate may be in the singular : ὄσσε δεδήει. Finally, the so-called Pindaric congruence may be mentioned : in Pindar we observe that sometimes the predicate is in singular, while the subject is in plural : ὕμνοι τέλλεται.

The subject in Ancient Greek is usually in nominative. Only in the construction of accusative and infinitive in the accusative, and in the construction of the genitive absolute—in the genitive. These constructions do not exist in Modern Greek.

The Predicate

The predicate is a verb or a noun united with the subject by the copula εἶναι. As many adjectives in Greek have but one ending for the masculine and feminine, the predicate frequently appears in the masculine form, while the subject is a feminine. Delbrueck explains this phenomenon (known only in Greek) in the following manner : The adjectives with one ending for two genders were originally substantives in ος; for example, λοίδορος signified originally slanderer, ἔωλος—the decline : ἔωλος δόξα = a fame which is a decline, that is, which is on the decline. For the same reason compound adjectives, of which the second part was a substantive, could not form a feminine : ῥοδοδάκτυλος, καλλίσφυρος. With regard to the adjectives in ιος,

ειος, αιος, and ιμος, which also cannot form a
feminine. Delbrueck thinks that as all adjectives
of this sort have more than two syllables, the
analogy of compound adjectives influenced them.
In poetry metrical necessity produced the same
effect; the ending of the feminine α or η is long,
while the ending of the masculine ος is short.

CHAPTER II

THE CASES

In Greek there were originally five cases, while in the primitive Indo-European there were eight. In Sanscrit we find them all: nominative, accusative, vocative, dative, genitive, ablative, instrumental, and locative. In Greek only traces have been preserved of the last three. We find the ending of the ablative in the adverbs in ως (from ωδ-s): καλῶς from καλῶδ-s (cf. the Latin od in the inscription of the Scipios: Gnaivod (later Gnæo) patre prognatus), of the instrumental—in the ending of the dative of the stems in A and O: οις and αις, and of the locative in the ending σι of the dative of the plural of the consonant-stems (cf. the ending of the locative in Sanscrit su).

The vocative is properly not a case. The Indian grammarians declared it to be an intercalary clause.[1]

The cases most fully in use are the nominative and the accusative. The genitive and the dative we see disappearing little by little. In the Romance languages and in English they have now ceased to exist. In Modern Greek the dative is supplied by

[1] Cf. above, p. 158.

εἰς with the accusative and also by the genitive.
In Ancient Greek the genitive sometimes takes the
place of the ablative and the dative—the place
of the locative and the instrumental of the primitive
language. The development from primitive Greek to
Modern Greek was as follows: ablative—genitive—
εἰς with the accusative; instrumental—dative—
με(τά) with the accusative; locative—dative or ἐν
with the dative—εἰς with the accusative.

As the nominative had often the same form as
the vocative, the nominative was united with the
vocative in addresses, for instance: ὦ ἄνδρες οἱ
παρόντες, or Ζεῦ πάτερ' Ἥλιός τε (*Iliad*, iii, 277).
This phenomenon is very old; we find it in Sanscrit:
Vājav Indraç ca! = O Vaju and Indra!

The Accusative

The accusative is called the case of the direct
object, for the noun, which depends directly on the
verbal notion, appears in this case. We say on the
verbal notion, for we mean not only verbs proper.
It is possible in Greek, as in many other Indo-
European languages, for substantives and adjectives,
which have become substantives, having the signification of a verbal notion to govern the accusative;
for example: ἐπιστήμονες ἦσαν τὰ προσήκοντα =
ἠπίσταντο τὰ προσήκοντα (Xenoph.), ἔξαρνός εἰμι τὰ
ἐρωτώμενα = ἐξαρνοῦμαι τὰ ἐρωτώμενα (Plato). The
accusative therefore is a supplement of the verbal
notion; it may be said, it expresses the extent of

the action. But there are also verbs which do not permit of such a supplement. On the other side it is an old phenomenon in the Indo-European languages, that after such verbs, the so-called ' intransitives,' in a certain signification the accusative may be used: μένω τινά (with the meaning ' to await,' not ' to remain '), γελῶ τινα (' to scorn,' not ' to laugh '). Cf. also the Pindaric expression πολὺνῦσε χρυσόν = it has rained much gold.

From the definition of the accusative it results also that this case signifies not only the object of the verbal notion, but also a direction or relation of the action of the subject towards something.[1] Thus we explain such accusatives in Greek as: 'Ολύμπια νικᾶν, πομπὴν πέμπειν, μάχην μάχεσθαι, κοιμᾶσθαι χάλκεον ὕπνον. Such use of the accusative is very old. In Sanscrit we find jīved vaiçyasya jivikām = he lives the life of a vaiçya. In Ancient Greek such an object could also be qualified by an adjective: ἄτιμος τὴν ταύτην ἀτιμίαν.

Further, by the accusative was expressed the extension of the verbal notion in space and time: γεγονὼς τριάκοντα ἔτη, Κῦρος ἔμεινεν ἡμέρας ἑπτά. The accusative of the direction answering the question whither ? also belongs to this category: θάλαμον κατεβήσετο (cf. in Latin, Romam proficisci).

---

[1] R. Blümel (in Indogermanische Forschungen, vol. 33) distinguishes : (1) an accusative of the space of command ; (2) an accusative of the direction ; (3) an accusative of the distance ; and (4) an accusative of the purpose.

But very early this construction was replaced by a preposition with the accusative.

The notion of the accusative as the case of relation is clearest in the construction named accusative of the inner object. It has existed in Sanscrit, but has disappeared very early. In Latin poetry it was used as a Grecism. But in Zend it was not less customary than in Greek. We find in Greek: ἀλγῶ τὴν κεφαλήν (Theocritus says in Doric: ἀλγέω τὰν κεφαλάν). Here, too, the verbal notion may be an adjective: βοὴν ἀγαθὸς Μενέλαος. To this category belongs the accusative of the measure: ποταμὸς εὖρος τριάκοντα πήχεων. It is true that Brugmann declares εὖρος, μῆκος, βάθος, etc., to be nominatives as apposition to the preceding substantives. Delbrueck explains the early disappearance of this accusative by the opposition of the instrumental; already Homer says instead of εὐρύτερος τοὺς ὤμους—εὐρύτερος ὤμοισιν. Brugmann's opinion is that, on the contrary, the accusative has in such cases ousted the instrumental.

Two accusatives also may depend on a verbal notion, one indicating an object and the other the duration of the action: πολιορκήσας Πάρον ἓξ καὶ εἴκοσι ἡμέρας, or an accusative of the inner object: φιλεῖν τινα παντοίην φιλότητα (*Odyssey*, ο, 245). Also two accusatives of the object may depend on one verbal notion: διδάσκω τινα μουσικήν. This is explained by what is called zeugma; two clauses are united into one: διδάσκω τινα + διδάσκω μουσικήν.

To this category belong expressions like ἀποφαίνω τινα τι, παρέχω ἐμαυτόν τι.

The immediate source of the accusative of the inner object is the ' accusativus græcus ': διδά-σκειν τινα μουσικήν being an established phrase, it was possible to go further and say: διδάσκεται τις μουσικήν. Hence came the idiom (according to Brugmann) of adding to passive verbs an accusative to express the object affected by the action, even when the verb in the active was not capable of being followed by accusatives of the whole and the part. We find, for example, in Xenophon: ἐτελεύτησαν ἀποτμηθέντες τὰς κεφαλάς. To the passive forms were associated the intransitive verbs, as in Homer: γέγηθε δε τὴν φρένα ποιμήν. By any of the participles this accusative wanted the adjectives also, as in Homer: πόδας αἱματόεις, φοξὸς τὴν κεφαλήν. Thus little by little the notion of the transmission of an action to an object passed over to the notion of some relation to this object. Here we have in consequence a return to the primitive use of the accusative (see above).

To the accusative of the inner object a qualifica-tion is often added: κακίστην δουλείαν δουλεύειν, ἥδιστον βίον ζῆν (= βιοῦν). But already in Homer the substantive is sometimes omitted and the verb is then determined by the adjective, which takes the place of an adverb: σμερδάλεον (κόναβον) κονάβησαν. Then followed the idiom of determining the verb by an adjective in the neuter accusative, where no substantive is omitted. Thus were formed the expressions: μέγα λέγειν, μανικὸν βλέπειν, ἡδὺ γελᾶν, μέγα φρονεῖν, etc. The plural also was often used: ὀξέα κεκληγώς, καλὰ πολιτεύεσθαι. It was in this way that in Modern Greek the neuter of the plural of the adjective took the place of an adverb. The adverbial use of the pronouns may be similarly explained: τοῦτο, τόσσον, τι, οὐδέν (τοῦτο χαίρει = ταύτην τὴν χαρὰν χαίρει). In Ancient Greek feminine adjectives also sometimes became adverbs: σχεδίην (πληγήν) τύψον (*Iliad*, v, 830).

The Genitive

As the accusative expresses the dependence of the noun on the verbal notion, the genitive expresses the dependence of one noun on another. The principal notion of the genitive is in the sphere or the category of something. One noun is thus determined by the other. The place of the genitive may therefore be taken by an adjective, a word whose natural function it is to determine another; instead of τεῖχος λίθου we may say τεῖχος λίθινον. Patronymica indeed were expressed in some of the Ancient Greek dialects by the genitive, and in others by adjectives: Δημοσθένης Δημοσθένους; cf. υἱὸς Σθενηλήϊος. In other Indo-European languages the latter manner prevailed. Also in Latin the addition of f(*ilius*) was usual; for instance, *Gai f(ilius)*. Only in Greek the patronymic was expressed by the genitive alone.[1]

It must be observed that in Greek the genitive may depend also on verbs; usually on those which indicate a partnership, for example: μετέχειν (τῆς λείας), μεταδιδόναι (τῶν χρημάτων). But here, too, an original dependence on the noun may be stated as the principal notion of the genitive. It was said: μετάδοσις τῶν χρημάτων or μέτοχος τῆς λείας. Thence the passage to μεταδιδόναι τῶν χρημάτων and μετέχειν τῆς λείας was natural.

In the same category may be mentioned the genetivus copiæ et inopiæ and the genetivus criminis. Similarly the genitive could depend on verbs indicating a striving or endeavouring, as γλίχεσθαι, ἐρᾶν, φιλοτιμεῖν, because one could say: ὁ πατρίδος ἔρως. Further, to the same category belongs the genitive dependent on the verbs indicating to perceive, to remember, to take care of something, not to remember, not to take care: αἰσθάνομαί τινος (from αἴσθησίς τινος, μιμνήσκω τινος (μνήμη τινος), ἀμελέω (from ἀμέλεια τινος), etc. This genitive is Indo-European: memini alicuius rei, sich *einer Sache* erinnern. Sometimes such verbs govern the accusative. A preponderance of the verbal character over the nominal must in this case be supposed. In the expression ἀκούω τινος we have the ablative genitive (cf. below). The genitive dependent on the verbs ' to eat,' ' to taste,'

---

[1] In Russian some family names in north-eastern Russia have the form of the genitive plural, for example : *Soukhíh, Pjányh.*

' to enjoy ' may be explained if we repeat that this case has the character of an adjective ; for instance, ἐσθίειν μόσχου is = ἐσθίειν μόσχειον κρέας. This genitive, too, was Indo-European: in old Saxon *wateres drinkan*, in Italian *mangiare del pane*, in Russian *napítsja wodý* (to drink *of the* water).

In Greek the genitive has also filled the place of the old ablative, especially in its principal notion, that is replying to the question : from what something is taken, or from what it is separated. The genitive appears dependent on verbs indicating a separation, and after the comparative and the superlative (genetivus comparationis) : ἀπέχω τινος, κωλύω τινος, ἀποστερέω τινος, ἄρχομαί τινος, μείζων τινος, κάλλιστον τῶν προτέρων φήος. In Modern Greek the place of this genitive is taken by the preposition ἀπό with the accusative. In the Greek dialects of Southern Italy this preposition is *api* : *to puli e caddio' pi to vorasi* = τὸ πωλεῖ(ν) (ἐστι) κάλλιο(ν) ἀπὸ τὸ ἀγοράζει(ν).

Further, the genitive of space and time may also be regarded as an ablative. The genitive of time was certainly Indo-European. Brugmann explains that the accusative indicated the extension of the time, the locative the time during which something has happened, and the genitive simply the date. Some scholars (Huebschmann, Siecke) have declared that this genitive (for example : νυκτός = in the night; cf. in German *nachts*) [1]

---

[1] As analogy to *tags*. They say : *tags über*.

is an adjective. For example, νυκτὸς ἦλθε = νυκτε-
ρινὸς ἦλθε. But the phrase might also be rendered:
he came from the side of the night. The genitive
in Greek would then replace an ablative (cf. in
Latin *noctu*). Night and day were regarded by the
astronomers as one totality—νυκτήμερον. The local
genitive has been explained by some scholars
(Brugmann, Hentze, La Roche) as a genitive
partitive; for example: ἔρχονται πεδίοιο. Delbrueck
originally believed that this genitive was in place
of the locative or the instrumental. Later he
thought that it was a ' genuine ' genitive (cf. his
Syntaktische Forschungen, iv, 44). But perhaps here,
too, the genitive might be explained as taking the
place of the ablative: ἔρχονται πεδίοιο = they
come from the plain. We must mention that in
Slavonic in such a case we have the instrumental:
in Russian *idút ravnínoï*. Also what is in Greek
genitive of time appears in Slavonic as the instrumental: in Russian *prišlí nóçju* = they came in
the night.

Lastly, the genitive in Greek had the place of the
ablative absolute (in old Slavonic and in German
the dative absolute).

As for the reason why in Greek the ablative had
its place taken by the genitive, Delbrueck has
pointed out that in Sanscrit the endings of both
cases in the singular of all the stems, with the
unique exception of the stems on *a*, were identical;
these endings are: *āh* (*bāl'ayāh*), *ah* (*vārinah*),

uh (*dātuh*), *eḥ* (*agnēh*), *ōḥ* (*satrōḥ*). To these endings corresponds in Greek *os*—the ending of the genitive singular of what is called the third declension. But if χάζεσθαι νηός was used, then by analogy χάζεσθαι κελεύθου would be possible. The uses of the genitive and ablative have little by little become confused and their limits broken down.

The Dative

While thus in Greek two old cases have coincided in the genitive, the dative represents as many as three cases: the dative, the locative, and the instrumental. Thus we may perceive in the forms employed in old Eleian, Arcadian, and Cyprian that the form of the locative is used for the dative, while in general in the first and second declension the contrary has happened. In the third declension the form of the locative is used for the dative in all dialects. In Homer besides the old instrumental used as a dative also the genuine form of this case on φι = *bhi* seems to exist. In Indo-European, according to Schleicher, besides the ending of the instrumental plural—*bhis*, we must suppose the form of the singular—*bhi*. But Hirt explains the Homeric ending φι as corresponding to the Gothic preposition *bi* = German *bei* = at. He thinks that βοῦς ἀγέληφι in Homer signifies ' an ox at the herd.'

Usually the dative is called the case of a wider object in contrast to the accusative, the case of the

nearest object. Kuehner defines the dative more
clearly as the case by which the person or the
thing is designed, for which something is being
done. Brugmann says more concisely: the dative
is the case of interest. Here the dativus commodi
and incommodi is conspicuous and also the dativus
finalis, designing a purpose. Here belongs also
(although one might also think of the instrumental)
the well-known Greek idiom, by which, if the predicate has the form of the perfect passive, the subject
appears in the dative: τί πέπρακται τοῖς ἄλλοις,
instead of τί ὑπὸ τῶν ἄλλων πέπρακται, or τοσαῦτά μοι
εἰρήσθω, instead of ὑπ' ἐμοῦ εἰρήσθω (*Lysias*, 24, 4).

Through this principal signification of the dative
is also explained the use of this case in dependence
on adjectives, signifying equality, resemblance, or
difference: ἴσος, ἀλίγκιος, ὅμοιος, ἀνόμοιος. Further,
of the adjectiva verbalia in τέος: ἐμοὶ πολεμητέον
ἐστίν. Finally, to this category belongs the dativus
ethicus and in Latin the dative, which might be
called reflective: *quid tibi vis* (in German cf. *das
hätte ich* mir *nicht gedacht !*).

It must be mentioned that some scholars do not
recognize this genuine dative as a grammatical
case and admit only its signification as a locative.
The original ending of the dative—*ai* is declared
to be a modification of the locative ending *i*. This
explanation of the dative seems indeed confirmed
by the very ancient forms χαμαί and *humi*. The
dativus locativus may be called also dativus

temporis, for it is used not only to signify place, but also time. As locative it is used to indicate where an object is (μυχῷ κλισίης) or the place to which it comes (πεδίῳ πέσεν). The dativus temporis remained longer in use. Such, for example, is τῇ προτεραίᾳ or 'Ολυμπίοις. This last example shows the possibility of a transition of a local case to a case indicating time : 'Ολυμπίοις = at Olympia, or = at the time of the Olympian games.

Also of persons the dative was used as a locative, but only in the plural. Nevertheless Delbrueck understands Θέμιστι in the phrase of Homer, ο, 88 : "Ηρη—Θέμιστι δὲ καλλιπαρήῳ—δέκτο δέπας—as a locative : from Themis, or at Themis. He proves this by a similar construction in Sanscrit.

In later times the locative was expressed by prepositions with the dative, not by the dative alone. Some genuine locatives are preserved nevertheless in classical Greek : 'Ολυμπίασι, 'Αθήνησι.

The instrumental had originally in Indo-European the signification of ' going together '; it was rather a casus sociativus. In Greek the dative as a successor of the instrumental has this signification only in Homer and very seldom in classical prose. We casually observe the transition to the later purely instrumental signification : ἥ νῦν δὴ Τροίηθεν ἱκάνεις νηΐ τε καὶ ἑτάροισι (λ 163). Here ἑτάροισι is sociative, but νηΐ—already a pure instrumental. Only the dative of αὐτός has preserved its sociative signification in the classical period as in Homer: ἀλλ' αὐτοῖς ἵπποισι καὶ ἅρμασιν ἆσσον ἰόντες = together with the horses (Ψ 8), αὐταῖς τριήρεσι = together with the ships. Further, designing sections of troops (cf. Xenophon, *Anab.* 7, 6, 29: θαρραλέως ἐφείποντο οἱ πολέμιοι καὶ πελταστικῷ. Closely related with this dative is the dative of circumstances: γυμνῇ τῇ κεφαλῇ, φαιδρῷ τῷ προσώπῳ, πολλῷ θορύβῳ, etc., and the dative of approach: ἕπεσθαι (in Latin *sequi* governs the accusative), ὁμιλεῖν, πολεμεῖν, μάχεσθαι τινι, etc. In Sanscrit these verbs are constructed with the instrumental: *bhrátā bhrátrā yuyudhé* = the brother fights with the brother.

In general the dative was governed by a verb or a verbal notion. But it happened also that the case was governed by a substantive or an adjective. This construction can be understood most easily when verbal substantives are used: τὴν τοῦ θεοῦ δόσιν ὑμῖν (Plato), ὑπηρέτης τοῖς νόμοις. Similarly the dative was used to mark a ' belonging to something,' or that something exists for something: ἧλοι ταῖς θύραις, γραμματεὺς τῇ βουλῇ (cf. in German: *leiblich* Dir *Geschwisterkind*, in Russian: *on* mnjé *drug* = he is my friend (' friend to me ').

Chapter III

THE VOICES OF THE VERB

Owing to the omission of the object many active verbs became used as intransitives. A very familiar example is ἐλαύνω, which originally signified to drive, to push, but later had the signification ' to move forward,' ' to ride,' and in general ' to advance.' This happened because of the omission of the object driven, for example, ἵππον.[1] Thus the verb ὑπάγω signifying originally ' to lead ' had already in Byzantine age the meaning ' to go.' Cf. in Modern Greek πηγαίνω, νὰ πάω, νὰ πᾷς—from νὰ ὑπάγῃς and νὰ πάγῃς, etc.

On the other hand, there were in Greek, as already in Indo-European, verbs having middle form, but active meaning: ἕπομαι, in Latin *sequor*, in Sanscrit *sácate*; κεῖται, in Sanscrit *śéte*; ἧσται, in Sanscrit *áste*. These are especially verbs expressing an emotion or a passion, as σέβομαι, ἄζομαι, ἄχνυμαι, χώομαι, and the future of many active verbs, as ἁμαρτήσομαι, φευξομαι, καμοῦμαι, etc. Delbrueck's explanation is that this phenomenon is due to a false generalization of such phenomena as βήσω = ' I will move,' βήσομαι = ' I will move

[1] It is well known that the same has happened also to the English verb ' to drive.'

forward,' that is 'I will go.' This explanation is not accepted by Hirt, because it remains unexplained why only single verbs followed this analogy, not all. Many active verbs had a middle future already in Indo-European times.

In the course of time the middle in Greek lost its reflexive value. Xenophon says ἑαυτῷ περιποιή-σοσθαι. Polybius uses ἀπαντῶμαι in the sense of ἀπαντῶ, Herodas—δεῖται in the sense of δεῖ. But already Homer—ὁρῶμαι in the sense of ὁρῶ. In Modern Greek the reflexive use of the middle is not known at all.

In Indo-European there were only two voices of the verb: the passive and the middle. This latter voice signified that the action had a relation to the subject. Thus this voice had properly two significations, the passive and the reflexive. Indeed, in Sanscrit there are passive forms only for the present stems, but these forms have developed from the present middle of the *ya*-class. Also in the Rigveda instead of this passive we find forms of the middle. In Slavonic real passive forms have never existed. They are supplied by the reflexive form of the verb (active + the reflexive pronoun) and in the past by the participle with the auxiliary verb. In Germanic languages this latter formation is preponderant. Also in Greek we have a proof of the original non-existence of the passive in the fact that the passive sense is for the most part expressed by forms historically middle. Only in the

aorist are there peculiar endings, ην and θην, for
the passive; but even these endings had not this
sense originally. They were active. The explanation
given by Delbrueck is as follows: The aorist
ἐδάμην (from δάμνημι) originally signified ' to become
tame.' If the author of this state is named, he
may appear either in the instrumental case or a
prepositional phrase may be used: ἐδάμη ὑπό τινος =
he became tame through somebody. An intransitive
verb is closely connected with a passive. This
form (the aorist passive) was naturally to hand and
ready when it was desired to create similar forms
from transitive verbs; for example, from τύπτω
it was possible and natural to form ἐτύπην on the
analogy of ἐδάμην.

During the development of the Greek language
little by little the passive signification of the middle
forms became preponderant. Finally, the middle
voice ceased *to exist at all*. The peculiar forms of the
future and aorist middle became obsolete. Often
the aorist passive appears instead of the aorist
middle.

In the passive construction the agent was for
the most part expressed by ὑπό with the genitive.
But other prepositions also were used: ἐκ τοῦ
κατ' ἄστυ βασιλέως τάδ' ἄρχεται (Sophocles, *Œdipus*,
col. 67). From the time of Polybius ἀπό with the
genitive usually appears (*I*. 34, 8: ἀπὸ τῶν θηρίων
ἀπώλλυντο). Homer uses also ὑπό with the dative:
ὑπ' Ἀργείοισι φέβοντο (*Il*. 11, 121).

CHAPTER IV

THE TENSES

It should be stated at once that the original function of the present, aorist, and perfect stems was not to indicate the time of the action, *when* something happened, but rather the manner of the action, *how* something happened.[1] We can thus understand, why from many stems some of the tenses cannot be formed. The present is wanting in stems signifying a momentary action, for the present by its nature signifies a lasting action. This was the case already in Indo-European. In Sanscrit *dhāv* = to run, expressing a lasting action, appears only in the present; similarly from the Greek θέω no aorist can be formed.

The Present

The present signifies a lasting action or state. But as present-stems appear in various forms, we must infer that there have been different shades in their significance. Delbrueck even supposes that the original signification of the present was not of a lasting, but of a beginning action.

[1] This fact is stated by G. Curtius in his *Erläuterungen zur griechischen Schulgrammatik*, 1875, p. 179.

180

There is no doubt that such a present existed in Indo-European. But as far as Greek, the matter must be left undecided.

As the present-stem in its original nature gave no indication at all of the time of action, so the present tense serves to indicate a condition or a continuous action not only in the present, but also in the past or in the future. In this connexion the historical present is well known. Delbrueck supposes that the use of this form was a special Greek acquisition made in later times, inasmuch as Homer mentions no use of it. Brugmann explains this by the epic style. However, after πάρος the present tense has even in Homer the signification of the past: πάρος γε μὲν οὔτι θαμίζεις (Σ 386). In regard to the use of the present as a future, individual present-stems have exclusively this signification. That is the case in verbs, the original signification of which is perfective, that is when this stem signifies a finished action; ' I find ' is perfective, ' I seek ' is imperfective. In Greek from perfective stems are formed the verbs εἶμι (= I will go), ἔδομαι (= I will eat), πίομαι (= I will drink). Having the form of a present these verbs have the signification of a future. But also in general the present may acquire the signification of a future, especially when the speaker is persuaded that an action or a state will ensue: εἰ αὔτη ἡ πόλις ληφθήσεται, ἔχεται ἡ πᾶσα Σικελία (Thucydides, 6, 91).

It has been observed that the present signifying a lasting action is wanting, if the verb signifies a momentary action. In these cases in Greek sometimes we find the *reduplication*. Well-known examples are: δίδωμι, τίθημι, (s)ίστημι. The root δο signifies ' to give something '; if for ever or for a time is left undecided. The reduplication was evidently used to strengthen the meaning and so to indicate that something is given for ever. A like supposition must be made of the other reduplicated verbs. The reduplication signified duration and repetition. Reduplication of the stem is especially found in words ending in σκω, as βιβρώσκω (βρο), διδάσκω (from δα = to make clear; cf. δάος, δάς, etc.).

The Future [1]

The original signification of the future in Indo-European was to express that somebody is *aiming* at something, and this signification we actually find in Sanscrit and Iranian. Brugmann cites a very clear example in Greek: ναυτικὸν παρεσκεύαζον, ὅτι πεμψουσιν ἐς τὴν Λέσβον (*Thucydides*, 3, 16). Then the temporal signification has developed.

The Imperfect and the Aorist

In Greek originally two tenses were used for narration: the imperfect and the aorist. The

[1] Cf. K. Magnian, *Le futur grec*, Paris, 1914.

difference was that the imperfect simply related, while the aorist signified an action *beginning* in the past. Thus in a narration both tenses may be used. The difference between them is most evident in the formule of the decrees of the Attic assemblies: ἔδοξε τῇ βουλῇ καὶ τῷ δήμῳ (the decree was brought about), ἡ δεῖνα φυλὴ ἐπρυτάνευε, ὁ δεῖνα ἐγραμμάτευε, ὁ δεῖνα ἐπεστάτει, etc. The fact that an artist made a work of art was expressed by the imperfect: Ἐχέδημός με ἐποίει, or by the aorist Παιώνιος ἐποίησε. In the first case the fact was narrated, and in the second it was barely stated. Here belongs also the so-called incohative aorist: Μίνως τῆς θαλάσσης ἐκράτησε (*Thucydides*, i, 4). As a form indicating the beginning of a state, the aorist appears in such expressions as ἥσθην = I am glad (properly: I began to be rejoiced) or ἐγέλασα = that is laughable (properly: I began to laugh at it). It is probable that we have here the original signification of the aorist, for in Sanscrit the tense is used almost exclusively in this way.

It is known that in some languages a supposition is expressed by the future or the future perfect. We say in French: *il sera parti* = I suppose that he has set off; or in German: *er wird abgereist sein*. In Modern Greek the aorist with the particle θά is used: θὰ ἀνεχώρησεν.

In Ancient Greek the aorist was used also to express a general sentiment (the ' gnomic aorist '). This is usually explained by the omission of such words as πολλάκις, or ἤδη, or in negative sentences, of οὔπω. Such words are, in fact, sometimes used with the gnomic aorist, and it was supposed that the Greek expressed a general experience by emphasizing the fact that the action in question had already happened. But this explanation will not serve for such sentences as: Time destroys all that is fair, ὁ χρόνος πᾶν καλὸν ἔφθειρεν. Bréal in his *Essai de sémantique* (p. 350) thinks that we have here a very old use of the aorist, dating from the time when this tense, like the perfect, would be applied to action in the present. The scholar thinks that the aorist in such sentences expresses only the manner of action.

The Perfect

The meaning of the perfect tense developed in Greek along the same line as in the Asiatic branch of Indo-European, that is in Sanscrit and in Avestan. The initial use of the perfect was to express the intensive nature of a condition. For example: τέ-θνηκε (from *θε-θνηκε) = dead—dead = totally dead. The reduplication marks the intensity. Later the perfect expressed an action done completely. From this the use of the perfect as a past tense naturally developed. Thus the perfect began to play the part of a rival to the aorist. We read in a papyrus of 160 before Christ (Pap. Louvre 327, line 23): εἶδον καὶ ἠξίωκα. Later the aorist gets the ascendant over the perfect, and in Modern Greek this tense has ceased to exist, having been in the period of the κοινή next to the aorist the tense of narration. The parallel use of both tenses has influenced the form of the perfect; it was modified in the direction of the aorist: instead of πεπαιδεύκασι—πεπαίδευκαν was formed (cf. ἐπαίδευσαν). In the modern καθαρεύουσα the perfect has been preserved to indicate an action done completely in relation to the present. The form also has been changed; instead of πεπαίδευκα—ἔχω παιδεύσει(ν). But this relation to the present has been a characteristic of the perfect ever since the time of Homer; it had always this relation to the present. While the latter signified that something now happens, the perfect signifies that something is now already done. Thus the perfect can sometimes take the place of the present: γέγηθα does not mean ' I have been glad,' but simply—I am glad. Some perfect stems have in Attic prose exclusively the present meaning: βέβηκα = I stand, μέμνημαι = I remember (cf. the Latin *memini*). The necessity arose of forming a past to correspond to these presents. This was done by the addition of the augment and by the use of a special ending. In this way the pluperfect came into being: βέβηκα—I stand, ἐβεβήκειν—I stood. It existed already in Sanscrit and in Avestan.

CHAPTER V

THE MOODS

The Indicative

The so-called 'modus irrealis' is expressed in Greek by the imperfect indicative with the particle ἄν or κέν. This may be explained by the analogy with verbs signifying 'it should be,' like ἔδει or ὤφελε. But this use of the indicative developed only later. Homer expresses the past irrealis also by the optative: καὶ νύ κεν ἔνθ' ἀπόλοιτο (*Iliad*, v, 311). So sometimes Herodot: εἴησαν ἄν (i, 2). This use of the optative is consistent with its signification as the mood of possibility. Cf. below. From the Hellenistic period onwards instead of ὤφελε as a particle, ὄφελον also was used, and this word, like εἴθε, was followed, not by the infinitive, but by a past tense of the indicative; for instance: ὡς ὄφελόν γε βρέγμα Φιλιππείης ἐξέπιον κεφαλῆς (*Anthologia Palatina*, ix, 519, 3). Wackernagel, quoting this instance, explains ὄφελον as a participium absolutum, like ἐξόν (instead of ἔξεστι— *Sprachliche Untersuchungen zu Homer*, p. 200).

The particles ἄν and κέν (κε, κα) differ both in their origin and in their use. The original form of the κα and κε(ν) was καν (cf. Hugo Weber, *Die*

dorische Partikel K A, Halle, 1864). This form is
found in inscriptions. Identical with κάν is the
Vedical particle *kám* (cf. Kuhn in *Hallische Allgem.
Litteratur-Zeitung*, 1846, ii, p. 846), the force of
which is to give emphasis (Kuhn and Benfey
translate ' certainly '—Böthling and Rothe in
German *wohl, ja*). But Delbrueck asserts that κα
with its indefinite signification comes from the
pronominal stem *ka*, not from *kám* (*Synt. Forschungen*, i, p. 88). One should perhaps translate:
at any time, at any manner. Osthoff (in *Z.G.d.T.*,
342) derives κάν from *sám* in Sanscrit (= *bene*;
cf. the German *wohl*). The particle ἄν is according
to Kuhn identical with the particle *ú* in Sanscrit.
But Delbrueck thinks that the identity is not
clear, and that ἄν has no parallel in Sanscrit. He
doubts even the identity of the Greek ἄν and the
Latin *an* supposed by Bopp, Grimm, Hartung, and
Pott. We can go no further than to remark that
ἄν is usually found in negative clauses and κέν with
the subjunctive mood in relative clauses. In
disjunctive clauses κέν is sometimes repeated,
while ἄν never is.

The Subjunctive

On the original signification of the subjunctive
opinions differ.[1] While J. M. Stahl and Delbrueck
suppose that its use was to express a desire, Hirt

[1] Cf. A. Walter, *Die Grundbedeutung des Conjunktivs im
Griechischen*, Heidelberg, 1923.

asserts that in its original signification it was a mood of the future. Brugmann supposes that already in the primitive language there existed three sorts of subjunctive: the voluntative (ἴδωμι), the deliberative (πῇ ἴω), and the prospective (ἴδωμαι). The most probable original use was the desire or purpose to do something. As the future tense expresses an action as aimed at, so the use of the subjunctive to refer to future time is quite natural. The deliberative subjunctive expresses the purpose in the form of a question—πῇ ἴω = where am I to go? Likewise the hortative use of the subjunctive may be explained: ἴωμεν = let us go. Still clearer is the original signification of the subjunctive as a mood of the purpose in subordinate clauses, especially in final clauses, where its use is obligatory. After the conjunctions ἵνα and μή the subjunctive must be used; after ὡς and ὅπως either the subjunctive or the future are allowed. Further, we see that the subjunctive occurs in conditional clauses with a futurist sense. In this case the particle ἄν, or κέν or κα is added: ἄν (= ἐὰν = *εἰ ἄν) ἐμὲ ἀποκτείνητε, οὐκ ἐμὲ μείζω βλάψετε ἢ ὑμᾶς αὐτούς. In temporal clauses also the subjunctive is used, if they relate to the future or express a purpose; then, too, the particles ἄν, κέν, or κά are used: ἐκέλευε τοὺς κήρυκας περιμένειν, ἄχρι ἄν σχολάσῃ (Xenoph., Anab. 2, 3, 2). Πάντες ἄνθρωποι, ὅταν (= ὅτε ἄν) περὶ ἀδικεῖν ἐπιχειρῶσιν, ἅμα καὶ τὴν ἀπολογίαν σκοποῦνται (Isocr., 21, 17).

The Optative

As the name indicates, the optative was a mood of desire.[1] This was its primitive use, but when united with the particles ἄν or κέν, the optative was used from the earliest period of Greek to express the idea of possibility. Either of these uses could very naturally have been developed from the other. Hirt's opinion is that the optative of possibility preceded the optative of desire. From the latter came what is called the optative of command, which sometimes is used in the place of the imperative, as for instance in an inscription of Elis: συμμαχία κ'ἔα (in Attic = ἄν εἴη) ἑκατὸν Ϝέτεα. From the optative of possibility came the use of the mood to express a suggestion or modified assertion, to which Delbrueck has given the name of the optative of futurity: εἴποι τις ἄν. Thus with the subjunctive the optative also has a relation to the future. This is the reason why in most languages it very early coincided with the subjunctive: in Latin,[2] in the Germanic languages, in Lithuanian, and in the Slavonic languages.[3] In Greek one may observe its gradual disappearance. (Cf. the

[1] Bopp ascribed to the syllable ιη, with which the optative is formed in Greek, the meaning of a desire. But in Sanscrit the corresponding syllable ya is not an independent root. The forms derived from this syllable belong to the root i = to go. For example, φέροιμι signifies properly ' I go to bear.' Cf. in English : I am going to do something.

[2] Cf. εἴην—sim (from *siem), εἶεν(τ)—sint (from *sient).

[3] In Sanscrit, on the contrary, the optative has supplanted the subjunctive.

Morphology above.) First it disappeared in subordinate clauses: in the 3rd century before Christ. After the 3rd century of our era it was quite obsolete in the living language.[1]

The well-recognized rule that an historic tense in the principal sentence must be followed by an optative in a subordinate sentence is observed by Homer only in the case of indirect questions. The rule is strictly observed only in classical Attic. In the Hellenistic period the rule is not predominant, and in later periods no attention to it is paid at all.

The Imperative

From the two circumstances that there is no positive indication of persons in the imperative and that in general few original suffixes can be distinguished (in Sanscrit only the second person singular in *a*, *dhi*, and *tad*, of which the latter is used also for the third person singular and plural), Delbrueck has inferred that the forms of the imperative had originally no relation to special persons, but were forms of the infinitive. Further, it is probable that there was at first an imperative only of the present, for in Sanscrit the imperative of the *s*-aorist is very rare and is even unknown

---

[1] On 100 pages of the text of Plato in the ed. Teubneriana we find 250 cases of the optative, while in the text of Strabo on 100 pages we meet only 76. In the whole New Testament we find only 67 cases. In Modern Greek the wish is expressed by transcription : ἤθελα νὰ πάγω = I would go.

in the Vedas and in prose. Only in Greek this imperative is frequent. Finally, Delbrueck infers from the observation of Grassmann that in the Vedas the negative *mā* (= μή) is always united with the not primitive subjunctive and never with the imperative, that the imperative expressed originally only a positive command, never a prohibition.

As the imperative forms were originally of the nature of the infinitive, it is quite natural that we should sometimes find the infinitive taking the place of the imperative. In Greek there is a distinction to be observed between the two: when the imperative is used, it is understood that the command must be carried out immediately; when the infinitive is used, the command is of a mere general nature; a course of action rather than a separate and distinct act is ordered: ἀναγράφειν τῶν πόλεων τὰ ὀνόματα—καὶ ἥτις ἄν ἄλλη συμμαχος γίγνεται— cf. in the same inscription, line 64: τὸ δὲ ψήφισμα ἀναγραψάτω ὁ γραμματεύς (Dittenberger, *Sylloge inscr.*, i, 80). If the infinitive imperative is used to command an immediate act, it is the aorist and not the present of the infinitive that is used.

Jolly, in his *Geschichte des Infinitivs*, pp. 158, 209, explains the imperative infinitive by the fact that the infinitive originally had the function of the final dative.

If the subject of the imperative infinitive has to

be expressed, the accusative is used. The reason for this may be supposed to be that some verb meaning ' to tell,' to bid,' or some impersonal verb has to be supplied. Cf. Hesiod, *Works and Days*, v. 389: γυμνὸν σπείρειν (to supply: δεῖ), but v. 430: θέσθαι πονησάμενος.

Chapter VI

THE DEPENDENCE OF CLAUSES

Although there is no doubt that originally clauses were put one beside the other without any formal subordination of one clause to another, nevertheless such subordination is very old and already Indo-European. Already in Sanscrit the pronominal stem *ya* serves as a means of subordination, as in Greek from Homer onward. On the other hand, we meet in Greek much later traces of the old παράταξις, although less frequently than in other languages: καὶ νῦν οὐ λέγει τις τὰ βέλτιστα ἀναστὰς ἄλλος εἰπάτω, instead of ἐάν τις μὴ λέγῃ, etc. (*Demosthenes*, 3, 18). In English we can say: they say, the enemy has invaded our territory, instead of: that the enemy, etc.

Subordinate clauses are either united with the principal clause by pronouns, by adverbs, or by the so-called conjunctions, or else special verbal forms and constructions are employed for this purpose; here we may mention the participles and the construction of the accusative with the infinitive, which is sometimes called the infinita locutio. In Modern Greek this construction does not exist, although in other Indo-European languages it is

193   N

still sometimes found. For instance, in German we can say: Ich sehe ihn schreiben (instead of " dass er schreibt "), and in Italian: gli dissi avere con me. (Cf. Goldoni, *La finta ammalata*, iii, 11.)

Although the Latin word *coniunctio* (a translation of the Greek συνδεσμός introduced by Aristotle) properly signifies ' a union,' the conjunctions are for the most part not uniting words. They are self-existent words expressing independent conceptions and certain relations between words and sentences. Thus they introduce the clauses expressing (1) the cause, (2) the consequence, (3) the condition, (4) the concession, (5) the purpose, (6) the time, and (7) the object (= transitive sentences).

Clauses expressing the cause are introduced in Greek by the following conjunctions: ὅτι, ὡς, ἅτε, ἐπεί, ἐπειδή, ἐπείπερ, ὅτε, and ὁπότε.

ὅτι (= ὅ, τι,—the neuter of ὅστις) was evidently a relative pronoun (as in Latin *quod* and the plural *quia*) and originally signified: the circumstance, that . . . Only little by little this meaning developed into ' *because* of the circumstance, that . . .' The construction was originally a παράταξις. The same may be said of ἅτε, οἷα δή, and ὡς; these conjunctions also were originally relative pronouns. The pronoun ἅ was united with the conjunction τε = and (originally = in Sanscrit *ca*, in Latin *que*, in Dorian *ka* = ὅτε, in Lesbian ὅτα). Homer does not yet know ἅτε as a conjunction. In the Attic period ἅτε was very usual; in the Roman period it became

obsolete. The conjunction ὡς corresponds to *yād*
in Sanscrit; the original Greek form was ἰωδς
(the ς is added on the analogy of the ending of the
nominative). From the time of Polybius (2nd
century before Christ) ὡς in its causative meaning
is obsolete.—῞Οτε and ὁπότε also were originally
relative pronouns.—᾽Επεί must be divided ἐπ-ει
(on ει see below), but the origin of this conjunction
found only in Greek is unknown. The ending δή
in ἐπειδή seems to express a locative like the
German *da*, which also has a causal meaning.—We
may add that the conjunction ἵνα (originally a local
adverb meaning 'where'; so still in Homer), although
usually expressing a purpose, sometimes as late
as the 1st century of our era had a causal meaning :
ἵνα παιδία λοιδορήσωσι τὸν ᾽Ελισσαῖον κατηρᾶτο
(= ὅτι ἐλοιδόρησαν; St. Paul, ad Timoth. ii, 12).

Clauses expressing a *consequence* are introduced
by ὥστε or ὡς. But in Homer ὥστε is not yet found.
Consecutive clauses are expressed in his poems by
the simple infinitive or a co-ordination with δέ,
οὖν, etc. ; for instance, νοῦσον ὦρσε κακήν, ὀλέκοντο δὲ
λαοί—instead of ὥστε ὀλέκοντο. The original signification of ὥστε was ' and how.' In the Roman period
for example, in Plutarch, we find ἵνα as well as
ὥστε. In Modern Greek we find a combination of
the two conjunctions ὥστε νά = ἵνα. Consecutive
clauses are introduced in Modern Greek by ὅπου =
where.

The conjunctions expressing a *condition* were in

Ancient Greek αἰ and εἰ (in Bœotian ἠ). Both had
originally a locative meaning. The German conjunction *wo* may be compared; although its proper
meaning is ' where,' it can also be used to mean ' if ';
for example, *wo er nicht kommt* instead of *wenn er
nicht kommt*. In Greek the locative ending of the
O-stem was ει (οἶκος—οἴκει) and of the A-stem αι
(Θῆβαι—γενής). Cf. in Latin *humi* and χαμαί.
To the αἰ corresponds *si* in Latin, but in Oskan *svai*.
Thus before αἰ another element originally existed
in Greek also; not before εἰ. We should await, it
is true, the spiritus asper *αἰ, but the spiritus lenis
had evidently taken its place by analogy with εἰ.
This latter conjunction is derived according to
Windisch (*Relativpronomen*, 329) from the anaphoric
pronominal stem *sva*. The original signification of
αἰ and εἰ is explained by Delbrueck (*Synt. Forsch.*,
i, p. 71): ' at the said place or in the said time.'

These conjunctions have therefore also a
temporal signification. Indeed, in all languages
conditional and temporal clauses stand in near
relation one to another.

The clauses with εἰ are divided into *a priori* and
a posteriori clauses. The former are properly the
conditional clauses. Here εἰ has the original signification ' of ' at any time, in some manner: εἰ τούτω
κεἡάβοιμεν, ἀροίμεθα κε κλέος ἐσθλόν = at any time
we take them, we will get great glory (*Iliad*, v,
273).

The *a posteriori* clauses with εἰ are indirect

questions: βάλλ' οὕτως, εἴ κέν τι φόως Δαναοῖσι
γένηαι = throw, thus wilt thou be a light to the
Danaoi = if thou wilt be a light to the Danaoi.
They were also sentences with εἰ, which were
properly principal clauses: ζ244: εἰ γὰρ ἐμοὶ τοιός δε
πόσις κεκλημένος εἴη = thus such a man would be
called mine. Here, however, it is possible that we
have to deal with a case of aposiopesis (cf. Delbrueck, *Syntaktische Forschungen*, i, 74). According
to Stahl (*Syntax des griech. Verbums*, 223, 1) εἰ
was 'thus, in such a manner'; cf. in Latin *sic*
(from *si-ce*), in German *so* = *wenn* (if). The
anaphoric signification 'thus' changed to the
relative, as in German *so‖wo* (p. 272).

If the condition referred to the future, the
predicate had to be put into the subjunctive, for
this was the mood of the future (see above). In
Attic and Ionic the particle ἄν was added, for this
particle had the meaning of 'perhaps' (above, p. 73).
It was usually contracted with the conjunction εἰ
to form ἐάν (εἰ + ἄν), for example, ἐὰν ἔλθη =
if (= perhaps) he will come. In Dorian dialects κα
corresponded to ἄν and in other dialects κεν or κε.

The negative in conditional clauses is not οὐ,
but μή. Instead of εἰ μή in some ancient dialects
we find other expressions: πλὰν μή (= except no)
at Delphi, πλὰν ἤ (= except than) in Kalymna and
Rhodos, πλὴν ἤ or πλὴν εἰ (= except, if), or ἐκτὸς εἰ
μή (= except if not) in Attica, ἐκτὸς αἰ (= except if)
in Lesbos.

In Modern Greek ἐάν is contracted to ἄν, and this has become the ordinary conditional conjunction quite independently of the question whether the condition relates to the future or the present or the past. Consequently, in opposition to Ancient Greek, after ἄν = ἐάν the indicative nowadays is used: ἄν θέλεις = εἰ θέλεις = if you will. Instead of ἐάν—χωρὶς νά is also said (= except that).

Concessive clauses were introduced by εἰ καί or ἐὰν καί or καὶ εἰ or κἄν = καὶ ἐάν. In Modern Greek they are introduced by ἄν καί, or ἀγκαλά = ἄν + the adverb καλά = well.

Clauses expressing a purpose (*the final clauses*) were introduced by ἵνα, ὅπως, or ὡς. The first of these conjunctions was properly a relative local adverb and in this signification is still met in poets; for example, in Sophocles: οὐχ ὁρᾷς, ἵν' εἶ κακοῦ. But it is supposed that the original signification was that of an instrumental; cf. in Sanscrit *yéna*, a word which also signifies ' where.' The original form of ὅπως was *σϜοδϙωδς = so, as; cf. the Gothic *sva*.

In Attic prose and the κοινή purpose was also expressed by τοῦ with the infinitive; in negative clauses by τοῦ μή. In Thucydides this infinitivus finalis occurs very often.

In general the negative final clauses were introduced by ἵνα μή, ὅπως μή, or the simple μή (cf. in Latin *ne*). After μή in this sense the future

indicative is sometimes used instead of the subjunctive (Aristoph., *Ecclesiazusai*, v, 495, μὴ
ὄψεται).

In Modern Greek final clauses are introduced
only by νά = ἵνα with the subjunctive; the negative
clauses by μή.

Temporal clauses were introduced by the
temporal adverbs: ὅτε, ὁπότε, ἡνίκα, ἐπεί, ἐπειδή,
ὡς, ἕως, πρίν, πάρος, ἔστε, ἄχρι, and μέχρι. If the
sentence concerned the future, the particle ἄν
was added and this was united with ὅτε, ὁπότε,
ἐπεί, and ἐπειδή to one word: ὅταν, ὁπόταν, ἐπάν
and ἐπήν, ἐπειδαν. In ὅτε, πότε, and ὁπότε we may
recognize relative stems: in ὅτε-jo, in πότε and
ὁπότε—qo (*qo-τε and *(s)oqoτε). Thus πότε means
'and how,' ὁπότε 'and so how.' Similarly in
German *so wie* has sometimes a temporal signification. The conjunction ἐπεί had originally the
signification whereon, as ἐπ = ἐπί signifies 'on'
and ει, as is already mentioned, is = 'where.'[1]
The conjunction ὡς corresponds to *yād* in Sanscrit.
The stem is *io* and the signification was 'how.'
The correlative was ὥς, from the stem *sō*. Also
ἕως is derived from the same stem *ἴο*. The original
form is found in Homer: ἧος, cf. in Sanscrit *yavat*
signifying 'how long?' or 'how great?' The word
πάρος, which occurs only in epic poetry, corresponds
to the Sanscrit *purás*.[2] Πρίν is perhaps a comparative

[1] Cf. in German *wo-r-auf*.
[2] Cf. in Slavonic *pŭrež*, in Russian *preždje* = before.

form of πρό as πρότερον, only with the other ending of the comparative—ιων. The original form of ἄχρι and μέχρι according to Fick (*Bezzenbergers Beiträge*, v, 168) was μ̥χρι. This word was a preposition and as such was, and still is, in Greek, followed by the genitive. As a preposition was followed by a case of a noun, so a whole sentence could follow μέχρι (= ἄχρι). In the same manner also ἔστε = ἐς-τε has become a conjunction. Another explanation has been suggested, according to which an ellipse is to be assumed and ἔστε regarded as an abbreviated form of ἐς ὅτε.

In Modern Greek only the following temporal conjunctions are preserved: ἐπειδή, ὅταν, ἕως, and πρίν. Joined to εἰς—ἕως also is used in a local sense: ἕως εἰς τὰ ὅρια τοῦ κόσμου. Πρίν is always used with νά, for in Ancient Greek πρίν was always followed by the infinitive and in Modern Greek the place of the old infinitive was taken by νά with the subjunctive.

The *relative* clauses were introduced by the relative pronouns ὅς and ὅστις. The latter containing the indefinite τις had a more general signification than the simple ὅς. In Homer and Herodotos an older idiom is preserved. We find the relative clauses sometimes introduced by the demonstrative ὅ, which in Herodotos appears also in the form ὅς. This word had originally the form *σος and is not to be confounded with the relative ὅς, which originally had the form *jος.

In Modern Greek instead of the relative the pronoun ὅποιος [1] of the indirect question with the article is used: ὁ ὁποῖος. Indeed, it is possible that the relative clauses were originally questions. We might infer this from the fact that in proverbial sentences in many languages the relative is placed before the demonstrative. In Sanscrit we have *jásja súchas, tásja bhájam* = he who loves, fears, but literally: whose is the love? Of him is the fear. In Latin: *quam quisque norit artem, in hac se exerceat.* In Russian: *čto posjéjal, to i zni* = What thou hast sowed, that thou must reap; properly: What hast thou sowed? That thou must reap.

Indirect questions also must be considered as subordinate clauses, since they appear as the object of the verb of the principal clause. In Ancient Greek they were introduced by the interrogative pronouns with the relative stem ὅ: ὅστις, ὁποῖος, ὁπόσος, ὁπότερος—and the adverbs ὅπου, ὁπότε, ὅπως, ὁπόθεν. Originally the subordination of such clauses was not felt at all. In Greek it was also possible to place the subordinate clause side by side with the principal without any sign of subordination; not only οἶδα τὴν γῆν, ὁπόση ἐστίν was said, but also οἶδα τὴν γῆν, πόση ἐστίν. In Modern Greek the latter form is even the only one possible and the old interrogatives are obsolete.

[1] The accent is changed by analogy with ὅστις. Properly it should be ὁποῖος. The accent is changed since the 12th century.

As we have already said, the place of subordinate clauses could in Greek be taken by the participles and by constructions with the infinitive. The use of the participles was due to a desire to unite the subject of the subordinate clause more closely with the principal verb: one clause could thus be formed instead of two; for example, ἥδομαι ἀκούων σου φρονίμους λόγους—I am glad *hearing* thy reasonable speech. Such a construction became the rule when the principal verb indicated an observation, or signified ' to point at ' or ' to announce.' If the two clauses have different subjects, the subject of the subordinate clause is put in the genitive, and the predicate in the form of a participle must be in agreement with it. This is the so-called absolute construction, which in primitive times was used in the Indo-European languages. In Latin it appears as ablative absolute. In the Slavonic languages as the dative. The Greek genitive absolute arose by analogy from the forms where the verb of the principal clause demanded the genitive. In impersonal expressions in Ancient Greek we find also the accusative absolute, but only in place of a causal clause; for example, εἰρημένον = because it was said (but cf. ἐξαγγελθέντων = when it was announced).

In Modern Greek there is an accusative absolute: φθάνοντας δὲ ἔμπρὸς εἰς ἔνα μεψίτι ἡ γραῖα τοῦ λέγει = when they came to a mosque, the old woman told him.

The accusative with the infinitive arose from the sentences, in which the verb could govern an accusative and an infinitive as an object. We find such sentences in all Indo-European languages: in Latin, *iubeo* [1] *eum abire*; in German, *ich heisse ihn gehen*; in Russian, *ja jewó priglasíl woití* = I invited him to come in.

[1] *Iubeo* corresponds in Sanscrit to the verb *yodhayami* = I move; thence the accusative.

APPENDIX

A LIST OF BOOKS ON THE HISTORY OF GREEK

P. KRETSCHMER, Einleitung in die Geschichte der griechischen Sprache, Göttingen, 1896.

OTTO HOFFMANN, Geschichte der griechischen Sprache[2], Leipzig (Göschen), 1916.

A. MEILLET, Aperçu d'une histoire de la langue grecque[3], 1930.

D. MAUROPHRYDES, Δοκίμιον τῆς ἱστορίας τῆς Ἑλληνικῆς γλώσσης, Smyrna, 1871.

G. HATZIDAKIS, Σύντομος ἱστορία τῆς Ἑλληνικῆς γλώσσης, Athens, 1915.

DI PEZZI, La lingua greca antica, Torino, 1888.

A. N. JANNARIS, The Greek Language, Boston, 1909.

J. WACKERNAGEL, Die griechische Sprache (in „ Die Kultur der Gegenwart " von Hinneberg I, Leipzig, 1907).

K. DIETERICH, Untersuchungen zur Gesch. der griech. Sprache, Leipzig, 1898.

A. THUMB, Die neugriechische Sprache, Feriburg i. Br., 1892.

E. KIECKERS, Historische griech. Grammatik (Göschen), Leipzig, 1926.

M. LAURAND, Grammaire historique grecque (Manuel des Études Gr. et Lat., Fasc. iii), Paris, 1921.

E. THOMAS, Studien zur griech. und lat. Sprachgeschichte, Berlin, 1912.

K. BRUGMANN und B. DELBRUECK, Grundriss der vergleichenden Grammatik der indogermanischen Sprachen[2], 1897–1916.

K. BRUGMANN, Kurze vergleichende Grammatik d. indogerm. Spr., Strassburg, 1902–4.

K. Brugmann und A. Thumb, Griech. Grammatik [4], München, 1913.

J. Wright, Comparative Grammar of the Greek Language[2], 1912.

Leo Meyer, Vergleichende Grammatik der gr. und lat. Sprache, Berlin, 1861–5, i[2], 1882–4.

Gustav Meyer, Griechische Grammatik[3], Leipzig, 1896.

V. Henry, Précis de la grammaire comparée du Grec et du Latin[2], Paris, 1896.

G. Curtius, Grundzüge der griech. Etymologie[5], Leipzig, 1879.

H. Hirt, Griechische Laut- und Formenlehre[2], 1912.

A. Thumb, Handbuch der griech. Dialekte, Heidelberg, 1909 (new edition by Kieckers, vol. i, 1932).

C. D. Buck, Introduction to the Study of the Greek Dialects[2], Boston, 1928.

O. Hoffmann, Die griech. Dialekte in ihrem histor. Zusammenhang, Göttingen, 1891–8.

R. Meister, Die griech. Dialekte, i–ii, 1882–9.

Fr. Bechtel, Die griechischen Dialekte, i–iii, 1921–4.

D. B. Monro, A Grammar of the Homeric Dialect[2], Oxford, 1891.

Day Seymour, Introduction to the Language and Verse of Homer, Boston, 1886, and Harvard Studies, 1892.

J. Wackernagel, Sprachliche Untersuchungen zu Homer, 1916.

K. Meisterhans-Schwyzer, Grammatik der attischen Inschriften[3], Berlin, 1900.

P. Kretschmer, Die Enstehung der κοινή, Wien, 1901.

A. Thumb, Die griechische Sprache im Zeitalter des Hellenismus, Strassburg, 1901.

Thackeray, A Greek Grammar of the Old Testament, 1909.

Wiener-Schmidel, Grammatik des neutestamentlichen Sprachidioms, 1894.

L. Radermacher, Neutestamentliche Grammatik[2], Tübingen, 1925.

A. T. Robertson, A Grammar of the New Testament.

R. Helbing, Grammatik der Septuaginta, Göttingen, 1907.

Witkowski, Prodromus grammaticae papyrorum Graecorum aetatis Lagidarum, 1897.

K. Foy, Lautsystem der griech. Vulgaersprache, Leipzig, 1879.

St. B. Psaltes, Grammatik der byzantinischen Chroniken, 1913.

G. Hatzidakis, Einleitung in die neugriechische Grammatik, Leipzig, 1892.

A. Thumb, Handbuch der neugriech. Volkssprache[2], Strassburg, 1910.

A. Thumb, Grammatik der neugriech. Volkssprache (Göschen), Berlin, 1915.

A. M. Dawkins, Modern Greek in Asia Minor, Cambridge, 1910.

Morosi, I dialetti greci della terra d'Otranto, 1870.

M. Deffner, Zakonische Grammatik, 1881.

W. Prellwitz, Etymologisches Wörterbuch der griech. Sprache[2], Göttingen, 1905.

E. Boisaq, Dictionnaire étymologique de la langue grecque, Paris, 1916.

B. Delbrueck, Syntaktische Forschungen 1–5, Halle, 1871–1888.

Jac. Wackernagel, Vorlesungen über Syntax, 1. 2, Basel, 1920–4.

Besides the literary monuments, an important source for the study of the evolution of Greek are the *inscriptions* and the *papyri*, i.e. ancient manuscripts found especially in Egypt and written on the fibres of the plant ' papyrus.'

Of the great collections of Greek inscriptions in the first place must be named the four volumes of the *Corpus Inscriptionum Graecarum* published by the Academy of Berlin under the direction of August Böckh in the years 1828–1859 (*CIG.*). Already in 1873 a new edition of inscriptions found in Attica, with the addition of those found after the publication of *CIG.*, was begun by Adolf

Kirchhof, *Corpus Inscr. Atticarum* (*CIA*). This work was finished in 1897. But in the year 1890 the Academy has undertaken also a publication of the inscriptions found in other parts of Greece (*IG.*). Since 1913 a cheaper edition is published.

Besides these general collections, other collections exist. By the student of *language* may be consulted : Collitz-Bechtel, Sammlung griechischer Dialektinschriften (four volumes, 1884–1910 ; supplements are published by Hofmann in 1911). Cauer, Delectus inscriptionum graecarum propter dialectum memorabilium [2] (1888). Solmsen, Inscriptiones graecae ad inlustrandas dialectos selectae (1910). The inscriptions on vases, being important for the study of the vulgar language, have been published by Dumont, Inscriptions céramiques de Grèce (1872), and by P. Kretschmer, Griechische Vaseninschriften (1894). Kaibel has published the metrical inscriptions (Epigrammata graeca ex lapidibus conlecta, 1878 ; supplements in Rheinisches Museum 34, pp. 181–213, and by Hofmann (1911)). The most ancient inscriptions are collected by Roehl (Inscriptiones Graecae Antiquissimae, *IGA*., and ' Imagines inscriptionum graecarum antiquissimarum ').

With regard to papyri, besides the special publications of the papyri preserved in the libraries and museums of many cities (Berliner Klassikertexte, The papyri of the British Museum), the student must also consult the ' Archiv für Papyrusforschung,' published under the direction of Winkler.